SHORTCUT 2
408 GROWTH QUOTES

by LINKED IN AND TOWN HALL ACHIEVER OF THE YEAR
EY NOMINEE ENTREPRENEUR OF THE YEAR
GRAND HOMAGE LYS DIVERSITY
WORLD TOP100 DOCTORS

Dr BAK NGUYEN, DMD

TO ALL THOSE LOOKING TO WALK THEIR LEGEND AND TO DISCOVER THEIRS GOD GIVEN POWERS

by Dr BAK NGUYEN

Copyright © 2021 Dr. BAK NGUYEN

All rights reserved.

ISBN: 978-1-989536-75-9

Published by: Dr. BAK PUBLISHING COMPANY
Dr.BAK 0094

DISCLAIMER

« The general information, opinions and advice contained in this medium and/or the books, audiobooks, podcasts and publications on Dr. Bak Nguyen's (legal name Dr. Ba Khoa Nguyen) website or social media (hereinafter the "Opinions") present general information on various topics. The Opinions are intended for informational purposes only.

No information contained in the Opinions is a substitute for an expert, consultation, advice, diagnosis or professional treatment. No information contained in the Opinions is a substitute for professional advice and should not be construed as consultation or advice.

Nothing in the Opinions should be construed as professional advice related to the practice of dentistry, medical advice or any other form of advice, including legal or financial advice, professional opinion, care or diagnosis, but strictly as general information. All information from the Opinions is for informational purposes only.

Any user who disagrees with the terms of this Disclaimer should immediately cease using or referring to the Opinions. Any action by the user in connection with the information contained in the Opinions is solely at the user's discretion.

The general information contained in the Opinions is provided "as is" and without warranty of any kind, either expressed or implied. Dr. Bak Nguyen (legal name Dr. Ba Khoa Nguyen) makes every effort to ensure that the information is complete and accurate. However, there is no guarantee that the general information contained in the Opinions is always available, truthful, complete, up-to-date or relevant.

The Opinions expressed by Dr. Bak Nguyen (legal name Dr. Ba Khoa Nguyen) are personal and expressed in his own name and do not reflect the opinions of his companies, partners and other affiliates.

Dr. Bak Nguyen (legal name Dr. Ba Khoa Nguyen) also disclaims any responsibility for the content of any hyperlinks included in the Opinions.

Always seek the advice of your expert advisors, physicians or other qualified professionals with any questions you may have regarding your condition. Never disregard professional advice or delay in seeking it because of something you have read, seen or heard in the Opinions. »

ABOUT THE AUTHOR

From Canada, **Dr. BAK NGUYEN**, Nominee Ernst and Young Entrepreneur of the year, Grand Homage Lys DIVERSITY, LinkedIn & TownHall Achiever of the year and TOP 100 Doctors 2021. Dr Bak is a cosmetic dentist, CEO and founder of Mdex & Co. His company is revolutionizing the dental field. Speaker and motivator, he wrote 72 books over 36 months accumulating many world records (to be officialized). His books are covering:

- **ENTREPRENEURSHIP**
- **LEADERSHIP**
- **QUEST OF IDENTITY**
- **DENTISTRY AND MEDICINE**
- **PARENTING**
- **CHILDREN'S BOOKS**
- **PHILOSOPHY**

In 2003, he founded Mdex, a dental company upon which in 2018, he launched the most ambitious private endeavour to reform the dental industry, Canada wide. Philosopher, he has close to his heart the quest of happiness of the people surrounding him, patients and colleagues alike. In 2020, he launched an International collaborative initiative named **THE ALPHAS** to share knowledge and for Entrepreneurs and Doctors to thrive through the Greatest Pandemic and Economic depression of our time.

In 2016, he co-found with Tranie Vo, Emotive World Incorporated, a tech research company to use technology to empower happiness and sharing. U.A.X. the ultimate audio experience is the landmark project on which the team is advancing, utilizing the technics of the movie industry and the advancement in ARTIFICIAL INTELLIGENCE to save the book industry and to upgrade the continuing education space.

These projects have allowed Dr Nguyen to attract interests from the international and diplomatic community and he is now the centre of a global discussion in the wellbeing and the future of the health profession. It is in that matter that he shares his thoughts and encourages the health community to share their own stories.

> "It's not worth it go through it alone! Together, we stand, alone, we fall."

Motivational speaker and serial entrepreneur, philosopher and author, from his own words, Dr Nguyen describes himself as a dentist by circumstances, an entrepreneur by nature and a communicator by passion.

He also holds recognitions from the Canadian Parliament and the Canadian Senate.

SHORTCUT 2
408 GROWTH QUOTES

by Dr BAK NGUYEN

INTRODUCTION
BY Dr BAK NGUYEN

CONCLUSION
BY Dr BAK NGUYEN

ANNEX
GLOSSARY OF Dr. BAK's LIBRARY
Dr. BAK NGUYEN

PART 1
GROWTH
Dr. BAK NGUYEN

PART 2
299 GROWTH QUOTES
Dr. BAK NGUYEN

PART 3
LAZY
Dr. BAK NGUYEN

PART 4
32 LAZY QUOTES
Dr. BAK NGUYEN

PART 5
THE POWER OF QUOTES
Dr. BAK NGUYEN

PART 6
77 FAMOUS QUOTES
Dr. BAK NGUYEN

IN THE MEMORY OF A DEAR FRIEND,
PAUL GALIPEAU.

INTRODUCTION
by Dr. BAK NGUYEN

Much has happened in so little time. This morning, I received the confirmation that **SHORTCUT volume 1, HEALING,** has just been published by both Apple Books and Amazon Kindle. That's book #93 and the first one published in over a month and a half. The last one published was **LAZY**, volume 2, **TO OVERACHIEVE EVERYTHING BEING LAZY**, at the end of May.

If I was looking for a *cheat* to reach 100 books written within 4 years, I got duped big time, by myself! I still have to compile the last 2 volumes of **THE POWER OF YES**. As I was looking for a cheat, the idea of compiling all of my quotes into a book surfaced.

Between compiling old books and writing new ones, I have to tell you how harder it is for me to rework on old stuff. It just feels like work. I do not have much satisfaction coming out of it. If it wasn't for my discipline, it would have taken years to even finish the first compilation of quotes.

As you all know, I am running against the clock: seven weeks and a half before the dateline of August 31, midnight, to celebrate the end of 4 years as a writer. So no, I have not slowed down, I just did not enjoy the process of recycling, correcting, and compiling, but not at all.

The funny thing is that I still have a few subjects to write about, some I have postponed for months by now. TIME MANAGEMENT, ORTHODONTICS, LEADERSHIP, INDUSTRY INTELLIGENCE are a few of those subjects. For some reason, my instincts pushed me to go the other way.

After a month, deep in the process of compiling, I was desperate. It was just a bad idea. But then, it was too late to go back. Compiling my own quotes, I was looking for 1000 quotes. Within 2 weeks, I was way over. At a certain point, I lost count... until the final recensus.

It is then that I gave an interview to a young podcaster who covered me since the beginning of my awakening, almost 4 years ago. He is a fan, that's for sure.

As he followed my journey, he raised the haters' question: at first, people were saying that I was cheating, hiring ghost authors to write for me. Then, they realized that no ghost author can write as much as fast and as diversely. They got buried under the accumulation of my titles published internationally by Apple Books, Amazon, and lately, Barnes and Noble.

The haters started to quiet down... or so I thought. Behind the silence, a new rumour was circulating: if I write that fast and that much, it must be crap! Smart people take months and years to write a book. I was insulting the idea of writing books every time that I announced a new book!

Well, I never faced the criticism in person, but as the question was raised, I could clearly see the *ugly face of jealousy* smiling back at me. As I said many times by now, I have accepted who I am and I am done apologizing for being better, smarter, and faster. I just do and I react to my results.

It is then that it hit me: that crazy endeavour that I took upon myself to compile all of my quotes, that was the ultimate answer to all of those thinking that I have no depth or writing crap.

I write about philosophy, about the **Energy Formula**, about medicine, business, emotional intelligence, midlife crisis, parenting... and I still have to defend myself in front of people who never pick up any of my books... or any books for that matter!?

Well, my answer this time will be one to remember. If I love to cheat and I am not shy from admitting that I will cut a corner when it is possible, for as long as I get to the finished line with acceptable results, I have in my hand what will shut all the naysayers down: my quotes and their abundance!

You cannot cheat writing quotes. A quote is not a rhetorical exercise. A quote is an affirmation and a formula put in the least number of words possible so it can be easily read, heard, and felt.

Well, with 2412 quotes, who will ever dare raise their voice about the depth of my writings and reflections anymore? I am sure that they will find another angle to criticize, but this one is shut for good.

I must admit that it felt good for the whole following evening. I got my revenge, soft and classy. By the next morning, I realized that feeling good was a huge understatement.

I write books, many books. This is my 94th. And yet, reading book is not trendy and is on a steep decline. People have a hard time focussing for the duration of a movie of 2 hours, how would they commit to a book requiring days and weeks of their time? Can I blame them? I am the same.

I do not read as much as I did myself. What I still read every morning are the quotes that I found on my news feed. That's it! I know that I am worth people's time, 30 seconds at a time. Let me rephrase that, I know that I can help and inspire many people. Quotes are my access to them.

Compiling my quotes, I did much more. I categorized them into categories, gave them a serial number, and included their origins (from which book it came from, so they can be easily be retraced within their original contexts).

After feeling good from the interview and sleeping a few nights on the understatement, I realized that I was breaking down the wisdom of my library of books into a different form, quotes, a form more accessible and more trendy.

But more than quotes, the compilation of my quotes was also the map to access all of my writing and sharing. If you read a quote and that is enough to help you, great! But if you read one that talks to you at a deeper level and you want to know more, you now have a shortcut to know which book to pick from the library!

> "To celebrate my new milestone,
> I found a hack to fit in today's trend!"
> Dr. Bak Nguyen

That's quote #2419. Now I understand why my instincts were pushing me to undertake that gigantic compilation. My body knew that it was the breakthrough that I needed. To fool my mind, it made me think that I was cheating. Actually, I was, not cheating, but hacking into a higher level!

So here it is, volume 2, starting a few hours after the publication of **SHORTCUT volume 1, HEALING**. **SHORTCUT volume 2** is all about **GROWTH**, now that we are out of our *Quest of Identity* and have started the healing process.

This time, **GROWTH** will be a little different. We will have access to 299 quotes of Growth. Then, as you start to know me well, I will share with you yet another *cheat*, 32 quotes (mindsets) on **LAZINESS**. Forget what you know about being lazy, these ones, you really want to know.

These 32 quotes are hacks that will propel you further and with ease through your journey.

And then, I will share with you the 77 famous Dr. Bak's quotes, the essential collection. As I do not expect any of you to read all of my books, one after the next, I made sure that those quotes you do not want to miss are coming back in each of the **SHORTCUT** volumes.

The chapter on the **POWER OF QUOTES** will cover 8 different famous quotes than those we spent time on in **SHORTCUT volume 1**. Shortcut, cheat, hack, lazy, these are the themes I jungle next to healing, growth, power, and success, not to forget happiness. Enjoy!

This is **Shortcut volume 2, GROWTH**. Welcome to the Alphas.

Growth happens at the giving end.

Dr. BAK NGUYEN

PART 1
"GROWTH"
by Dr. BAK NGUYEN

From the day that we are born, we are looking for growth. Anger is growth, sex is growth, desire is growth. But then, society happened and we were forced into a mold. Whatever your story, into that mold, we were forced in, forged and clipped to fit the convention and the expectations.

What will be forced in will change the course of our evolution. Depending on the severity of the forging and its timing, it will affect our own understanding of who we are and how we see ourselves. Well, this is what they will like us to believe.

Sooner or later, we will all resume back to our original path. The longer was the wait, the more difficult will be the awakening, but it always happens.

"We are all born happy. Somehow, we are all looking to find what we were born with…"
Dr. Bak Nguyen

And that's quote #2420. Put differently, we were born in harmony with nature, with our talents and preferences. Then, they came in, even with the best of intentions, forced their will and history to **civilized** each of us with passion, determination, and fire. This is why I said that we all need healing.

And sooner or later, we will awake from the lies and start our Quest of Identity, looking for happiness, for freedom. That was step one and day one. That was the **AWAKENING**.

In **SHORTCUT volume 2**, we are walking the 2nd phase of this journey, the **GROWTH**. Growth, not in the primary sense of eating to survive but growth in the sense of sorting the truth from the lies. Excuse me, let me reformulate that: Growth sorting our truth from the lies.

Society and **Conformity** had their agenda. What they forced into us were lies, or at best, their version of reality, not the truth. On that matter, there is no absolute truth, just our perception of what we see, feel and understand.

> "And this is where we all got screwed, looking at life through the sunglasses that we received from education, culture, and religion."
> Dr. Bak Nguyen

That's quote #2421. So if the healing process was the coming to the realization that we were set on an artificial path, one that could not lead us to our happiness, one deprived of liberty and personal satisfaction, we first understood the lies and made peace with our past. To understand that we are broken, to acknowledge the long-overdue denial, and to pass the revolt stage, that's **HEALING**.

Now, we still need to move forward. So what is next? These filters and sunglasses that we received from **Conformity**, how do we get rid of them? Well, it gets even messier. If some of the lies were obvious and easy to spot, most take roots much deeper and have grown as part of who we are, of what defines us. All those filters are called mindsets.

One by one, we need to revisit each of these mindsets of ours and see which are still relevant and which are simply unneeded burdens. So no, GROWTH is not only the quest for new information, if it was that simple, we would not be making such a big deal of out it.

GROWTH is the internal fight that we all have to face, putting on trial what we knew and what we learnt to cherish as our own. Identity, truth, values, knowledge, and wisdom, we will have to revisit everything that we know, weighting them in the balance of what makes us happy.

On that, we each have our own reality and the only way to sort the truth from the lies is through feeling. Feeling, not thinking.

> "Thinking is where the filters all applied."
> Dr. Bak Nguyen

And here is quote #2422. But feeling is not simple either. At this stage, there is no feeling good, since we are sorting out our own building blocks, sorting the core of our nature and the burdens. To me, what is not helping me to move ahead, to move faster, are burdens.

Medals, values, loves ones, we will all be deeply hurt as we are going through the sorting process. To help cope with the self-inflicted pain, I kept from my past only **GRATITUDE**.

> "Gratitude is the only past with a future."
> Dr. Bak Nguyen

And I sorted out everything with that in mind. This is more than healing and accepting, now we have initiated the process of Identity. Each filter, values, and mindset that we are getting rid of will feel as if you are peeling a layer of skin. The roots, the chains, and the flesh will be screaming and smelling.

Some will do it slowly, trying to understand every inch of the process. They will feel every inch and second of the painful process, but even worse, will have doubt whispering in their ear at each step of the way.

I prefer the band-aid mentality, to rip it off promptly, leaving a clean and sharp pain but one I can clearly identify. Until now, there is no happiness in the process. But as we are peeling away the filters and the skins, feeling comes with more ease.

For the first time since… for as long as we can remember, we feel something new, something real. That's our body reacting to life, without filters. After the initial shock, what feels good is your reality. What does not, as good as it might sounds and looks are burdens and relics from another life.

To help me through the walk of pain, I bypassed my mind and logic since it is mainly where doubts lay. As I start feeling raw and unfiltered truth and I restart the education process of taking in information, feeling it, understanding it, and finally, sorting it.

I wish I could say that quickly I felt better. That isn't the case. Through the GROWTH process, I needed to heal at each step of the way, in parallel. To do that when you are still neighbouring your anchors (family and friends) is an impossible task.

This is why I said that the **QUEST OF IDENTITY** is one that you must take alone, when you feel ready. As you are sorting out your truth and preferences, you are welcome your past back into your life, only this time, they won't be defining you nor influencing what you should feel.

Be grateful and remember who gave you what. Then, feel and acknowledge what you are feeling in their presence. That's your answer! Before your mind has the time to kick in, acknowledge what you are feeling as your own and only truth. Now you know what to do.

As the sorting process begins, you will be leaving more than you wished behind. Now you have holes in your heart and a *bypassed mind*. These voids that you are feeling are the forces that will be pushing you to look ahead for answers. Resist the temptation of thinking, see the world with your heart and body, through feeling.

"The great thing about feeling is that it does not lie."
Dr. Bak Nguyen

That's the 2423rd quote. Sometimes you will love the feeling, other times, you will hate it with all of your being. Acknowledge that truth. That is one that you do not have to justify nor apologize for. That is who you are.

Please be careful, what I just showed you was how to take in the information and stimuli, not to push into any action nor decision of any kind. Feel and understand first. Then to act, you will need to deal with who you were!

At the crossroad of what you are now feeling and who you were is GROWTH in the sense of this book, this journey. Before, all you knew was the truth and reality you have inherited. Now, you have your own to balance it with.

Since we still live in society and have to behave in harmony and respect, our GROWTH is happening as we keep moving in Society but now, knowing our truth from the lies. You will be surprised by the change.

Most of the time, we will keep doing what we did before for a long moment, just like nothing ever happened but the internal acknowledgment of how we feel.

As we keep moving forward, but now sorting the facts and truth under a different light, we are slowly emerging as who we were destined to be. If you took the time to experience that change internally before reacting externally, you now have an undeniable advantage: you have insights and privileged information on the system you are living in. Now that you know who you are, moving forward won't be a problem anymore. You know the way as your heart is the compass.

And your mind? Since you put it on mute for that long (in the awakening and healing process) welcome it back, by not in control, leave the feelings in their rightful places. Have your mind to serve your heart and you will have aligned the stars in your favour. Then, have your mind to execute your desires and to serve as ambassador to society and you are now a kind force of your own.

This is GROWING. Growing as you are healing at the same time. Growing while you are keeping your head low to avoiding waves of change before you really know who you are and where you want to go.

And the voids you have created, leaving your burdens behind, well, those are the opportunity of the adventure ahead, as you will be looking to feel the voids. But something else has changed too.

As you have resisted the temptation to replace quickly those burdens and values you left behind while acknowledging **GRATITUDE**, your heart and mind both have grown bigger, allowing more and more stimuli to come in.

Feel and see what is worth keeping… and before it becomes painful again, revisit often the values and mindsets you have accepted. What was true yesterday may be only a half-truth today.

Following next are mindsets and leverage to help you through your journey. If I said that this quest, you have to take alone, well, I will also add that you do not to be on your own.

Know who you are first, feeling your truth, and soon enough, you can have company and help to leverage yourself to the next level.

This is **Shortcut volume 2, GROWTH**. Welcome to the Alphas.

Growth happens at the giving end.
Dr. BAK NGUYEN

PART 2
"299 GROWTH QUOTES"
by Dr. BAK NGUYEN

0985
FROM SYMPHONY OF SKILLS
"As much as I can't do much about it, I don't care"
Dr. Bak Nguyen

0986
FROM SYMPHONY OF SKILLS
"If you are swimming against the tides, you can't swim for long before a monster tide will break you."
Dr. Bak Nguyen

0987
FROM SYMPHONY OF SKILLS
"Be a breeze rather than a storm!"
Dr. Bak Nguyen

0988
FROM SYMPHONY OF SKILLS
"Never walk away with a pure loss."
Dr. Bak Nguyen

0989
FROM SYMPHONY OF SKILLS
"Be a breeze first and slowly grow into a storm."
Dr. Bak Nguyen

0990
FROM SYMPHONY OF SKILLS
"Don't think, feel. You have to give in to grow!"
Dr. Bak Nguyen

0991
FROM SYMPHONY OF SKILLS
"No mind can outgrow itself without connection with an equal or superior mind."
Dr. Bak Nguyen

0992
FROM SYMPHONY OF SKILLS
"Do it, and do it now! the day is still young!"
Dr. Bak Nguyen

0993
FROM SYMPHONY OF SKILLS
"Our roots do not grow in the ground, and we do not take pride in holding a stand."
Dr. Bak Nguyen

0994
FROM SYMPHONY OF SKILLS
"As we need always to move forward, we need to stay light."
Dr. Bak Nguyen

0995
FROM SYMPHONY OF SKILLS
"Do yourself a favour, don't get attached,
to things, to people, to the past!"
Dr. Bak Nguyen

0996
FROM SYMPHONY OF SKILLS
"To confuse function and title would be
the beginning of the end."
Dr. Bak Nguyen

0997
FROM SYMPHONY OF SKILLS
"We learn as we share and we grow as we learn."
Dr. Bak Nguyen

0998
FROM SYMPHONY OF SKILLS
"Sharing is like a sport,
it's getting easier with daily practice!"
Dr. Bak Nguyen

0999
FROM SYMPHONY OF SKILLS
"One's story can only begin
when one's Quest of Identity is over."
Dr. Bak Nguyen

1000
FROM SYMPHONY OF SKILLS
"Thank God, I am an entrepreneur,
and entrepreneurs do not grow from the roots… "
Dr. Bak Nguyen

1001
FROM SYMPHONY OF SKILLS
"To think is not to act."
Dr. Bak Nguyen

1002
FROM LEADERSHIP, PANDORA'S BOX
"Our focus today will define our meal tomorrow."
Dr. Bak Nguyen

1003
FROM LEADERSHIP, PANDORA'S BOX
"Pride is self-awareness of one's intelligence
without the presence of a purpose for the greater."
Dr. Bak Nguyen

1004
FROM LEADERSHIP, PANDORA'S BOX
With humility, intelligence is the sharpest tool that we have at our disposal. With Humility!
Dr. Bak Nguyen

1005
FROM LEADERSHIP, PANDORA'S BOX
" Innocence is the ignorance of those safeguards for survival."
Dr. Bak Nguyen

1006
FROM LEADERSHIP, PANDORA'S BOX
" Innocence will allow us to go to the edge and jump without fear, without hesitation, not overthinking the unknown."
Dr. Bak Nguyen

1007
FROM LEADERSHIP, PANDORA'S BOX
" The difference lies only in the size of each heart."
Dr. Bak Nguyen

1008
FROM LEADERSHIP, PANDORA'S BOX
"Feed your heart, not your doubts."

Dr. Bak Nguyen

1009
FROM LEADERSHIP, PANDORA'S BOX
"Everything once started little. Littleness, not smallness."

Dr. Bak Nguyen

1010
FROM LEADERSHIP, PANDORA'S BOX
"The last win, the past win, is simply a stepping stone, not a cornerstone."

Dr. Bak Nguyen

1011
FROM LEADERSHIP, PANDORA'S BOX
"Don't spend too much of your life looking for a name. Spend time forging your name in the fire of life."

Dr. Bak Nguyen

1012
FROM IDENTITY, ANTHOLOGY OF QUESTS
"Unity is one's inner peace."
Dr. Bak Nguyen

1013
FROM IDENTITY, ANTHOLOGY OF QUESTS
"Templates make it easier to start but harder to really be. "
Dr. Bak Nguyen

1014
FROM IDENTITY, ANTHOLOGY OF QUESTS
"Stay hungry to feed, not to eat!"
Dr. Bak Nguyen

1015
FROM IDENTITY, ANTHOLOGY OF QUESTS
"We are what we eat. "
Dr. Bak Nguyen

1016
FROM IDENTITY, ANTHOLOGY OF QUESTS
"To see, to reach, to grow. The recipe has 3 acts."
Dr. Bak Nguyen

1017
FROM IDENTITY, ANTHOLOGY OF QUESTS
"To think is just the beginning.
To be, we'll have to do."
Dr. Bak Nguyen

1018
FROM IDENTITY, ANTHOLOGY OF QUESTS
"In your Quest of Identity, chose carefully who are
your allies, but even more carefully,
who you chose to defy!"
Dr. Bak Nguyen

1019
FROM IDENTITY, ANTHOLOGY OF QUESTS
"Of all the pasts, gratitude is really the only one
that one can safely look at without turning
into a ghost or a statue of salt!"
Dr. Bak Nguyen

1020
FROM IDENTITY, ANTHOLOGY OF QUESTS
"If you sleep through the day, you will still
have to make your journey, only with the moon
instead of the sun as a guide."
Dr. Bak Nguyen

1021
FROM IDENTITY, ANTHOLOGY OF QUESTS
"Midlife crisis is one's forced rebirth."
Dr. Bak Nguyen

1022
FROM IDENTITY, ANTHOLOGY OF QUESTS
"You are always right!
Think it, act upon it and it will be!"
Dr. Bak Nguyen

1023
FROM IDENTITY, ANTHOLOGY OF QUESTS
"On the other side, you are on our own,
but you don't have to be alone!"
Dr. Bak Nguyen

1024
FROM IDENTITY, ANTHOLOGY OF QUESTS
"Be hungry to feed, not to eat, since one will grow you and the other will make you fat!"
Dr. Bak Nguyen

1025
FROM IDENTITY, ANTHOLOGY OF QUESTS
"I told you, knowledge is no wisdom.
Be careful of what you feed yourself with!"
Dr. Bak Nguyen

1026
FROM IDENTITY, ANTHOLOGY OF QUESTS
"Whatever your mind helps you feel,
are no real emotion nor sensation, since there are
no connections, therefore, no growth!"
Dr. Bak Nguyen

1027
FROM IDENTITY, ANTHOLOGY OF QUESTS
"Have love. Fear to lose. Grasp it hard!
That's the carrot we fed on for years!"
Dr. Bak Nguyen

1028
FROM IDENTITY, ANTHOLOGY OF QUESTS
"Remember, hunger and greed
are not the same."
Dr. Bak Nguyen

1029
FROM IDENTITY, ANTHOLOGY OF QUESTS
"You have to realize that what you are seeking lays beyond the mirror, not in front of it!"
Dr. Bak Nguyen

1030
FROM IDENTITY, ANTHOLOGY OF QUESTS
"To avoid destitution, never look down neither at your feet neither at others'. Looking up, always, will be your journey and by extension, your Destiny."
Dr. Bak Nguyen

1031
FROM IDENTITY, ANTHOLOGY OF QUESTS
"Problems started the minute we started labeling. Unfortunately, that was the first verse."
Dr. Bak Nguyen

1032
FROM PROFESSION HEALTH
"You are not alone and you don't have to be. But mark my words, you are on your own!"
Dr. Bak Nguyen

1033
FROM PROFESSION HEALTH
"Feed yourself with the credit
and leave your medals home."
Dr. Bak Nguyen

1034
FROM PROFESSION HEALTH
"We will learn, we will get better and we will thrive
and surf the victory, sooner or later."
Dr. Bak Nguyen

1035
FROM INDUSTRIES' DISRUPTORS
"The vibe of positivity is sustainable
as we keep sharing and growing."
Dr. Bak Nguyen

1036
FROM INDUSTRIES' DISRUPTORS
"When people tell me no, I say thank you!"
Dr. Bak Nguyen

1037
FROM INDUSTRIES' DISRUPTORS
"The day we stop learning, that day,
the rise has stalled and the fall is waiting."
Dr. Bak Nguyen

1038
FROM INDUSTRIES' DISRUPTORS
"The day you cease learning is the day
your fall starts occurring."
Dr. Bak Nguyen

1039
FROM INDUSTRIES' DISRUPTORS
"To learn on the way is the ultimate wisdom."
Dr. Bak Nguyen

1040
FROM INDUSTRIES' DISRUPTORS
"You can't gain momentum nor experience
while you are waiting."
Dr. Bak Nguyen

1041
FROM INDUSTRIES' DISRUPTORS
"Don't be cheap with your creativity.
The more you give, the better you'll become."
Dr. Bak Nguyen

1042
FROM INDUSTRIES' DISRUPTORS
"The making of a hero is made by the kind of responsibilities he puts on his shoulders."
Dr. Bak Nguyen

1043
FROM INDUSTRIES' DISRUPTORS
" ... and how can the world benefit from it?"
Dr. Bak Nguyen

1044
FROM INDUSTRIES' DISRUPTORS
"Being responsible is profitable! "
Dr. Bak Nguyen

1045
FROM INDUSTRIES' DISRUPTORS
"Greed has outgrown fear, by much, very much!"
Dr. Bak Nguyen

1046
FROM INDUSTRIES' DISRUPTORS
"Nothing will last if we do not entertain and exchange in a daily renewal."
Dr. Bak Nguyen

1047
FROM INDUSTRIES' DISRUPTORS
"To be humble does not mean to be docile. It means to listen."
Dr. Bak Nguyen

1048
FROM INDUSTRIES' DISRUPTORS
"The grinding is unique, and yet, the sweat all follow the same path: keep moving and renewing."
Dr. Bak Nguyen

1049
FROM INDUSTRIES' DISRUPTORS
"Don't wait and be open."
Dr. Bak Nguyen

1050
FROM CHANGING THE WORLD FROM A DENTAL CHAIR
" Stubbornness can be a quality
in the shoes of an entrepreneur."
Dr. Bak Nguyen

1051
FROM CHANGING THE WORLD FROM A DENTAL CHAIR
"The humility to serve and the wisdom to recognize
both strengths and flaws will make the difference."
Dr. Bak Nguyen

1052
FROM CHANGING THE WORLD FROM A DENTAL CHAIR
" It's up to you to fit in."
Dr. Bak Nguyen

1053
FROM CHANGING THE WORLD FROM A DENTAL CHAIR
"There is no absolute truth. The truth is not the same
for people of different vibes and values."
Dr. Bak Nguyen

1054
FROM CHANGING THE WORLD FROM A DENTAL CHAIR
" Technology allows me to free myself from procrastination."
Dr. Bak Nguyen

1055
FROM CHANGING THE WORLD FROM A DENTAL CHAIR
" If you can think of it, do it!"
Dr. Bak Nguyen

1056
FROM THE POWER BEHIND THE ALPHA
" Generosity before strength, flexibility before intelligence."
Dr. Bak Nguyen

1057
FROM THE POWER BEHIND THE ALPHA
" Sharing made me grow into who I am. Winning is now a side effect."
Dr. Bak Nguyen

1058
FROM THE POWER BEHIND THE ALPHA

" Respect to me is not a civility but a privilege.
The privilege to have someone worthy
of my attention and dedication. "

Dr. Bak Nguyen

1059
FROM THE POWER BEHIND THE ALPHA

" To be humble is to know who you are and
what you are not. But it started by knowing and
accepting who you are."

Dr. Bak Nguyen

1060
FROM THE POWER BEHIND THE ALPHA

"Pointing fingers is a dangerous and traitorous game.
It mainly shows one's own true nature."

Dr. Bak Nguyen

1061
FROM THE POWER BEHIND THE ALPHA

" The only way to avoid the shock is to be grateful."

Dr. Bak Nguyen

1062
FROM MOMENTUM TRANSFER
" The energy footprint you leave as you move around is called a vibe. Your vibe. That's your signature. "
Dr. Bak Nguyen

1063
FROM MOMENTUM TRANSFER
" The EYE of my momentum is the depth of awareness of what I can achieve. "
Dr. Bak Nguyen

1064
FROM MOMENTUM TRANSFER
"The path of least resistance is always the answer."
Dr. Bak Nguyen

1065
FROM MOMENTUM TRANSFER
"To keep an open mind is the only way to outgrow yourself."
Dr. Bak Nguyen

1066
FROM HYBRID
"Feelings and thoughts alone are not enough.
You need energy to fuel them all."
Dr. Bak Nguyen

1067
FROM HYBRID
"To keep moving forward and building
on top of a momentum, make it fun!"
Dr. Bak Nguyen

1068
FROM HYBRID
"I do not care about the label. I simply don't have
time for them and too lazy to learn about them."
Dr. Bak Nguyen

1069
FROM HYBRID
"The secret to my speed is to keep thing
as simple as possible."
Dr. Bak Nguyen

1070
FROM HYBRID

"Only if we feed, we may grow.
Hunger is Life reminding us of our evolution."

Dr. Bak Nguyen

1071
FROM HYBRID

"To feed is Greed. So are growth and desire.
Nothing is more natural."

Dr. Bak Nguyen

1072
FROM HYBRID

"We were made stronger, and stronger.
We grew following our heart and our body."

Dr. Bak Nguyen

1073
FROM HYBRID

"In the Quest of Identity, we based everything
with values from the past."

Dr. Bak Nguyen

1074
FROM HYBRID
"FEAR is from the head, while GREED is from the lower body, the instincts."
Dr. Bak Nguyen

1074
FROM HYBRID
"We are running a race, against ourselves, our own laziness and insecurities."
Dr. Bak Nguyen

1075
FROM HYBRID
"To avoid that paralysis, we must keep our mind and heart clear, to understand the real race we are competing in, the race of Life, the race to better ourselves."
Dr. Bak Nguyen

1076
FROM HYBRID
"Since my Mind is the smallest part of my Whole… I wonder why I was craving all the thing."
Dr. Bak Nguyen

1077
FROM REBOOT, TO GROW FROM MIDLIFE CRISIS
"If we accumulate too much gas, the same car will become a bomb waiting to explode."
Dr. Bak Nguyen

1078
FROM REBOOT, TO GROW FROM MIDLIFE CRISIS
"To enhance attraction, add Fear in the mix."
Dr. Bak Nguyen

1079
FROM REBOOT, TO GROW FROM MIDLIFE CRISIS
"Testosterone, attention and sex. In a word, Empowerment."
Dr. Bak Nguyen

1080
FROM LEVERAGE COMMUNICATION INTO SUCCESS
"We feel as much as the effort we put in. It's not karma, it's biology."
Dr. Bak Nguyen

1081
FROM LEVERAGE COMMUNICATION INTO SUCCESS
"The day people do not know what to expect from you, that day you will have gained true freedom of action."
Dr. Bak Nguyen

1082
FROM LEVERAGE COMMUNICATION INTO SUCCESS
"To keep the hope and the positivity and not to side with hate and fear, one must resist to close up."
Dr. Bak Nguyen

1083
FROM LEVERAGE COMMUNICATION INTO SUCCESS
"Know yourself, know who you are talking to, and start leveraging."
Dr. Bak Nguyen

1084
FROM FORCES OF NATURE
"Eventually, what was once intimidating, is now déjà vu."
Dr. Bak Nguyen

1085
FROM FORCES OF NATURE
"We often face the challenges we deserve… "
Dr. Bak Nguyen

1086
FROM FORCES OF NATURE
"Control is one of the greatest of power.
Power over oneself."
Dr. Bak Nguyen

1087
FROM FORCES OF NATURE
"One needs to replenish without slowing down."
Dr. Bak Nguyen

1088
FROM FORCES OF NATURE
"To face truth is a necessary evil to keep one humble
and prepare one to eventually face God."
Dr. Bak Nguyen

1089
FROM FORCES OF NATURE
"Emotions are hormonal responses.
The recipe and the dosage are our identities."
Dr. Bak Nguyen

1090
FROM FORCES OF NATURE
"To fly, one must be light. to speed, one must cut the dead weights. Those luckiest had nothing to cut!"
Dr. Bak Nguyen

1091
FROM FORCES OF NATURE
"If the sun sets behind the mountain of inertia, I know that I am walking in the right direction."
Dr. Bak Nguyen

1092
FROM FORCES OF NATURE
"All awakenings are brutal. with time, we are simply expecting its effects."
Dr. Bak Nguyen

1093
FROM FORCES OF NATURE
"I use the light of truth to make sure that I am polishing myself and not my shield."
Dr. Bak Nguyen

1094
FROM FORCES OF NATURE
"Ambitions, not Expectations."
Dr. Bak Nguyen

1095
FROM THE LEGEND OF THE DRAGON HEART
"Dragons are invisible because as they mastered a shape, they unlearn it to master a new one."
Dr. Bak Nguyen & William Bak

1096
FROM THE BOOK OF LEGENDS, VOLUME 1
"I am discovering the next step as I talk, as I walk, as I write."
Dr. Bak Nguyen

1097
FROM THE BOOK OF LEGENDS, VOLUME 1
"The super chicken is a dead end from the evolutionary standpoint."
Dr. Bak Nguyen

1098
FROM THE BOOK OF LEGENDS, VOLUME 1
"Leadership and an Alphaness are gifts received at birth. Nevertheless, to shine they need to be accepted and polished continuously."
Dr. Bak Nguyen

1099
FROM THE BOOK OF LEGENDS, VOLUME 1
"It is all a matter of projection and perspective. The difference is the ripple effect of their influence."
Dr. Bak Nguyen

1100
FROM THE BOOK OF LEGENDS, VOLUME 1
"A journey of discovery and of curiosity, that's the way of the dragon."
Dr. Bak Nguyen

1101
FROM THE BOOK OF LEGENDS, VOLUME 1
"Evolution is a matter of choice and awareness."
Dr. Bak Nguyen

1102
FROM THE BOOK OF LEGENDS, VOLUME 1
"I didn't want to do the job. I was simply keeping my momentum going... on the back burner..."
Dr. Bak Nguyen

1103
FROM THE BOOK OF LEGENDS, VOLUME 1
"Patience doesn't mean to wait."
Dr. Bak Nguyen

1104
FROM THE BOOK OF LEGENDS, VOLUME 1
"Humility is the acceptance of who we are, truly. This is no pretension since it is the truth."
Dr. Bak Nguyen

1105
FROM SELFMADE
"I synchronized myself with nature, with the universe."
Dr. Bak Nguyen

1106
FROM SELFMADE
"It's not in the mirror that you will find your true reflection but in the eyes of those you meet and connect with. it is called worth."
Dr. Bak Nguyen

1107
FROM SELFMADE
"Believing in tomorrow starts with your choices, today!"
Dr. Bak Nguyen

1108
FROM SELFMADE
"To mentor is a privilege, to be mentored is a blessing."
Dr. Bak Nguyen

1109
FROM SELFMADE
"To fly. I put hope as the EYE of my tornado. Suddenly, my storm was growing bigger and more powerful and yet, I was calmer."
Dr. Bak Nguyen

1110
FROM SELFMADE
"It takes courage to keep showing up, defeat after defeat, but until I run out of time, it's not over!"
Dr. Bak Nguyen

1111
FROM SELFMADE
"The only way to grow is to evolve. To evolve, we need to adapt, endlessly."
Dr. Bak Nguyen

1112
FROM SELFMADE
"When it's not your mess, it's a pure opportunity to help, learn and grow, without pain nor resistance, since it is emotionless!"
Dr. Bak Nguyen

1113
FROM SELFMADE
"I use my emotions to find opportunities."
Dr. Bak Nguyen

1114
FROM SELFMADE
"With the right attitude, half of the solution is already there."
Dr. Bak Nguyen

1115
FROM SELFMADE
"Find your worth and you will be too busy to stop at road bumps or to talk about it."
Dr. Bak Nguyen

1116
FROM SELFMADE
"That's how I move forward, with my head cold and my heart open. I am at your service, I am Dr. Bak."
Dr. Bak Nguyen

1117
FROM SELFMADE
"it's normal to be insecure facing the unknown and the new, but to choose to fear it is a choice, one with a heavy burden."
Dr. Bak Nguyen

1118
FROM SELFMADE
"Move swiftly, you might get burn but you won't get scared."
Dr. Bak Nguyen

1119
FROM SELFMADE
"To eclipse doubt, expand your comfort zone."
Dr. Bak Nguyen

1120
FROM SELFMADE
"The first question was not who am I,
but what do I want?"
Dr. Bak Nguyen

1121
FROM SELFMADE
"The only change one should expect is the one
that he will do on himself."
Dr. Bak Nguyen

1122
FROM SELFMADE
"So I learn to bet on myself!"
Dr. Bak Nguyen

1123
FROM SELFMADE
"Nothing will last forever.
But everything can be renewed."
Dr. Bak Nguyen

1124
FROM SELFMADE
"The only party you are forever stuck with is yourself."
Dr. Bak Nguyen

1125
FROM SELFMADE
"Practicing is the ultimate way to learn."
Dr. Bak Nguyen

1126
FROM SELFMADE
"It's never easy to change,
but it's not that hard to move forward."
Dr. Bak Nguyen

1127
FROM THE RISE OF THE UNICORN
"Do not wait for the competition to challenge you,
challenge your own position."
Dr. Bak Nguyen

1128
FROM THE POWER OF YES VOLUME TWO
"People and emotions are the building blocks
of every adventure, of every journey."
Dr. Bak Nguyen

1129
FROM CHAMPION MINDSET
"Most of the time, the right answer to what to stand for will not be one you've decided, but one decided for you!"

Dr. Bak Nguyen

1130
FROM CHAMPION MINDSET
"One does not change. One evolves."

Dr. Bak Nguyen

1131
FROM HOW TO WRITE A BOOK IN 30 DAYS
"Heart to heart is genuine."

Dr. Bak Nguyen

1132
FROM KRYPTO
" Feel to learn. This time, it wasn't that expensive."

Dr. Bak Nguyen

1133
FROM KRYPTO
"It is easier to clean the flood without emotion and when our feet are dry on land."

Dr. Bak Nguyen

1134
FROM THE BOOK OF LEGENDS, VOLUME 2
"I've learnt to never depend on anybody, especially to keep my MOMENTUM up."
Dr. Bak Nguyen

1135
FROM THE BOOK OF LEGENDS, VOLUME 2
"An ungrateful heart is shrinking day after day, until it becomes a rock."
Dr. Bak Nguyen

1136
FROM POWER, EMOTIONAL INTELLIGENCE
"What I feel often tells me what to do."
Dr. Bak Nguyen

1137
FROM POWER, EMOTIONAL INTELLIGENCE
"To feel is our most basic skills. We were born with that skill."
Dr. Bak Nguyen

1138
FROM POWER, EMOTIONAL INTELLIGENCE
"No matter the answer, look for the HOW and the WHY, not the WHAT."

Dr. Bak Nguyen

1139
FROM HORIZON VOLUME ONE
"The only control we have is to control how we will be reacting."

Dr. Bak Nguyen

1140
FROM HORIZON VOLUME ONE
"The day you think that you are the best, that is the beginning of the end."

Dr. Bak Nguyen

1141
FROM THE POWER OF YES, VOLUME 1
"Yes, is how everything started, anything and everything."

Dr. Bak Nguyen

1142
FROM THE POWER OF YES, VOLUME 1
"I opened my spirit and I embraced my calling, not letting anything behind."

Dr. Bak Nguyen

1143
FROM THE POWER OF YES, VOLUME 1
"To grow, one must open up.
It is impossible to open up and not to feel.
Feel to grow."

Dr. Bak Nguyen

1144
FROM THE POWER OF YES VOLUME 3
"To find the answers you seek, stop talking and start walking your path."

Dr. Bak Nguyen

1145
FROM THE POWER OF YES VOLUME 3
"Do yourself that favour, stay light, stay open, stay dynamic, you are alive!"

Dr. Bak Nguyen

1146
FROM HOW TO NOT FAIL AS A DENTIST
"The longer you will take to learn to count, the longer, people and the system will do the math for you…"

Dr. Bak Nguyen

1147
FROM HOW TO WRITE A SUCCESSFUL BUSINESS PLAN
"It is when you have invested everything and that you have nothing left that the real growth kicks in."

Dr. Bak Nguyen

1148
FROM MINDSET ARMORY
"My loyalty lays in the experiences and the soul of things."

Dr. Bak Nguyen

1149
FROM MINDSET ARMORY
"Share and don't get attached."

Dr. Bak Nguyen

1150
FROM HORIZON VOLUME TWO
"Be open, and your mind will have a chance to see the world, past, present and future."

Dr. Bak Nguyen

1151
FROM MINDSET ARMORY
"Before one could talk and walk,
one must listen and master with patience."

Dr. Bak Nguyen

1152
FROM MINDSET ARMORY
"We are the results of the sum of our decisions,
average with the outside environment
surrounding us."

Dr. Bak Nguyen

1153
FROM HUMILITY FOR SUCCESS
"The main confusion is to define Humility based on
how the world sees us."

Dr. Bak Nguyen

1154
FROM HUMILITY FOR SUCCESS
"The power of Humility is to stop pretending,
doubting and to start walking your legend."

Dr. Bak Nguyen

1155
FROM HUMILITY FOR SUCCESS
"It is the elasticity of one's mind that will determine how far one will go and how long one will last, even after his demise."
Dr. Bak Nguyen

1156
FROM HUMILITY FOR SUCCESS
"The goal of the journey is not to touch the finish line. It is to get better at it while having fun."
Dr. Bak Nguyen

1157
FROM HUMILITY FOR SUCCESS
"Medals won't help much since I won't have much time looking in the mirror!"
Dr. Bak Nguyen

1158
FROM HUMILITY FOR SUCCESS
"Looking to beat my score of yesterday kept the elasticity of my mind and even improve it."
Dr. Bak Nguyen

1159
FROM HUMILITY FOR SUCCESS
"Every time that I meet with a fan,
I grow a little more humble."
Dr. Bak Nguyen

1160
FROM MASTERMIND
"The Quest of Identity is mostly a lonely path.
Everyone has to walk it, and no one can do
this one with you."
Dr. Bak Nguyen

1161
FROM MASTERMIND
"Choices and consequences, it is as simple."
Dr. Bak Nguyen

1162
FROM PLAYBOOK INTRODUCTION VOLUME 2
"There is no free money.
You are always earning your money."
Dr. Bak Nguyen

1163
FROM PLAYBOOK INTRODUCTION VOLUME 2
"Being rich is a mindset and a different way
to see life and its opportunity."
Dr. Bak Nguyen

1164
FROM PLAYBOOK INTRODUCTION VOLUME 2
"Respect, openness and the desire to always move forward are the keys to find your mentors."
Dr. Bak Nguyen

1165
FROM PLAYBOOK INTRODUCTION VOLUME 2
"There is a world of difference between working for a salary, saving money and making money. And the key differences are TIME and LEVERAGE."
Dr. Bak Nguyen

1166
FROM PLAYBOOK INTRODUCTION VOLUME 2
"There is no free money, remember that!
But some money will require more work than others."
Dr. Bak Nguyen

1167
FROM PLAYBOOK INTRODUCTION VOLUME 2
"Run fast enough, you will be flying, keeping the same mindset to be open to adapt, being respectful and aware of your environment."
Dr. Bak Nguyen

1168
FROM PLAYBOOK INTRODUCTION VOLUME 2
"The more one does, the more imperfect he becomes. But then, his worth starts to rise."
Dr. Bak Nguyen

1169
FROM PLAYBOOK INTRODUCTION VOLUME 2
"We do, we do, and we earn."
Dr. Bak Nguyen

1170
FROM PLAYBOOK INTRODUCTION VOLUME 2
"With a rival involved, you do not have to worry about keeping focus anymore!"
Dr. Bak Nguyen

1171
FROM AMONGST THE ALPHAS, VOLUME 2
"The universe is abundant. The truth is vast and contains many realities."
Dr. Bak Nguyen

1172
FROM AMONGST THE ALPHAS, VOLUME 2
"Forgiveness heals all wounds."
Dr. Bak Nguyen

1173
FROM AMONGST THE ALPHAS, VOLUME 2
"The future is always brighter, if not,
what is the point of talking about it?"
Dr. Bak Nguyen

1174
FROM AMONGST THE ALPHAS, VOLUME 2
"With evolution, fear is growing obsolete."
Dr. Bak Nguyen

1175
FROM AMONGST THE ALPHAS, VOLUME 2
"To move up the ladders, you must step on the past,
a solid past, and keep looking at the next step.
Your head is aiming at the horizon."
Dr. Bak Nguyen

1176
FROM AMONGST THE ALPHAS, VOLUME 2
"I will just say that we can be better."
Dr. Bak Nguyen

1177
FROM AMONGST THE ALPHAS, VOLUME 2
"We are part of our legacy until we fill it
with our choices and achievements."
Dr. Bak Nguyen

1178
FROM AMONGST THE ALPHAS, VOLUME 2
"The smallness of a mind is to accept
solely what it understands."
Dr. Bak Nguyen

1179
FROM AMONGST THE ALPHAS, VOLUME 2
"Running out of fear and anger,
I became one with my beast."
Dr. Bak Nguyen

1180
FROM AMONGST THE ALPHAS, VOLUME 2
"Through hope and inspiration, I bargained
my way out of anger and revolution."
Dr. Bak Nguyen

1181
FROM AMONGST THE ALPHAS, VOLUME 2
"To save yourself from pain, don't get attached."
Dr. Bak Nguyen

1182
FROM AMONGST THE ALPHAS, VOLUME 2
"The first real power I ever discovered is the SERENITY OF VELOCITY."
Dr. Bak Nguyen

1183
FROM AMONGST THE ALPHAS, VOLUME 2
"Velocity allowed me the time to heal."
Dr. Bak Nguyen

1184
FROM AMONGST THE ALPHAS, VOLUME 2
"Perfection is a lie, and control, an illusion."
Dr. Bak Nguyen

1185
FROM AMONGST THE ALPHAS, VOLUME 2
"Do not revolt. The goal is to evolve without resistance."
Dr. Bak Nguyen

1186
FROM AMONGST THE ALPHAS, VOLUME 2
"Creativity works in many ways. One of my favourite is to react to the world as I see it."
Dr. Bak Nguyen

1187
FROM AMONGST THE ALPHAS, VOLUME 2
"We all, somehow, learnt to leave our past behind,
not to turn into statues of salt."
Dr. Bak Nguyen

1188
FROM AMONGST THE ALPHAS, VOLUME 2
"To keep learning, that's the youth, that's the power!"
Dr. Bak Nguyen

1189
FROM SUCCESS IS A CHOICE
"To gain perspective is to open up,
not to turn our back on what was."
Dr. Bak Nguyen

1190
FROM SUCCESS IS A CHOICE
"Be first to have later. Have first, and
you will never be anything more."
Dr. Bak Nguyen

1191
FROM SUCCESS IS A CHOICE
"Help people, don't judge people.
You'll be surprised how powerful you can be."
Dr. Bak Nguyen

1192
FROM SUCCESS IS A CHOICE
"Knowledge change behaviours, behaviours translate
into actions, and actions have consequences."
Dr. Bak Nguyen

1193
FROM SUCCESS IS A CHOICE
"To play is not safe,
but with education, it can be safer."
Dr. Bak Nguyen

1194
FROM SUCCESS IS A CHOICE
"If you want safe, embrace knowledge.
Then embrace flexibility to succeed."
Dr. Bak Nguyen

1195
FROM SUCCESS IS A CHOICE
"To clearly see what defence plays like
in everyday's life, look at your wagons."
Dr. Bak Nguyen

1196
FROM SUCCESS IS A CHOICE
"Personal finance is personal. It is for you to handle it,
understand it and drive it."
Dr. Bak Nguyen

1197
FROM THE 90 DAYS CHALLENGE
"One day, one entry."
Dr. Bak Nguyen

1198
FROM THE 90 DAYS CHALLENGE
"Find accountability, make it fun. You've just leveraged your pride into doing what you need to do."
Dr. Bak Nguyen

1199
FROM THE 90 DAYS CHALLENGE
"Discipline is not a religion, it is a choice and a lifestyle."
Dr. Bak Nguyen

1200
FROM THE 90 DAYS CHALLENGE
"To think of doing something takes more energy than to actually doing it!"
Dr. Bak Nguyen

1201
FROM THE 90 DAYS CHALLENGE
"Even if numbers can lie, trends never do."
Dr. Bak Nguyen

1202
FROM THE 90 DAYS CHALLENGE
"To identify a trend, have your record straight and on a daily basis! Especially the personal data."
Dr. Bak Nguyen

1203
FROM 90 DAYS CHALLENGE
"Trend and tenacity make us what we are."
Dr. Bak Nguyen

1204
FROM RISING
"Rising, the pain is mostly external if you had a visceral hunger, to begin with. If you didn't, the pain would be both external and internal.
The real pain, in the internal one."
Dr. Bak Nguyen

1205
FROM RISING
"Beliefs are from the heart."
Dr. Bak Nguyen

1206
FROM RISING
"To me, what matters is the result,
and what I've learnt along the way."
Dr. Bak Nguyen

1207
FROM RISING
"This is not about following, but about sharing!"
Dr. Bak Nguyen

1208
FROM RISING
"To breakdown the unknown, jump enough times,
so the presence of the variable becomes
your referral and fix value."
Dr. Bak Nguyen

1209
FROM RISING

"Not all challenges are made equal. Some will raise your legend, some others will bury you alive. Jump and sort, do not forget the sorting part."

Dr. Bak Nguyen

1210
FROM RISING

"It is your time to rise! And don't forget to have fun along the way, that's the only way to last."

Dr. Bak Nguyen

1211
FROM AFTERMATH

"To grow, one must open their mind. That the start, to not stay stuck, one also has to open their heart."

Dr. Bak Nguyen & William Bak

1212
FROM AFTERMATH

"As the best defence is offence, the most powerful strengths are kindness, generosity and flexibility."

Dr. Bak Nguyen

1213
FROM AFTERMATH
"Being genuine and open
have very strong side effects."
Dr. Bak Nguyen

1214
FROM AFTERMATH
"I didn't need wings to fly, just to cut my anchors."
Dr. Bak Nguyen

1215
FROM RELEVANCY
"First know who you are. Then, learn to know who
the other person is, then, and only then, talk."
Dr. Bak Nguyen

1216
FROM RELEVANCY
"Relevancy is ahead, never behind."
Dr. Bak Nguyen

1217
FROM MIDAS TOUCH
"We do and hope for the best."
Dr. Bak Nguyen

1218
FROM MIDAS TOUCH
"Do, hope and welcome the possibilities."
Dr. Bak Nguyen

1219
FROM THE POWER OF DR
"All tensions, as the rise flatten,
will turn into pressure."
Dr. Bak Nguyen

1220
FROM THE POWER OF DR
"Whatever you think you are, you are right!"
Dr. Bak Nguyen

1221
FROM THE POWER OF DR
"Sooner or later, everyone will have to embrace the
journey to their identity, That one,
you have to do alone."
Dr. Bak Nguyen

1222
FROM TORNADO
"From each encounter, there is always something to learn. If not from the other party, then, from ourselves."
Dr. Bak Nguyen

1223
FROM TORNADO
"Don't kill your Momentum with expectations."
Dr. Bak Nguyen

1224
FROM TORNADO
"Choosing silence and ignorance will turn friction into opposition."
Dr. Bak Nguyen

1225
FROM EMPOWERMENT
"In what you believe, on what you bet, the words you are using are defining your reality."
Dr. Bak Nguyen

1226
FROM EMPOWERMENT
"Glory. It starts with hope, then become glory and will transform into pride."
Dr. Bak Nguyen

1227
FROM EMPOWERMENT
"Self-motivation is resilience while self-inspiration is narcissism."
Dr. Bak Nguyen

1228
FROM EMPOWERMENT
"Do not stand for too long neither on defeat nor glory, these will just rust your soul."
Dr. Bak Nguyen

1229
FROM EMPOWERMENT
"To build from the difference got me my wings back."
Dr. Bak Nguyen

1230
FROM THE MODERN WOMAN
"It is not balance that you should aim for, but harmony."
Dr. Bak Nguyen

1231
FROM BOOTCAMP
"To me, gratitude is a way to look back without vertigo."
Dr. Bak Nguyen

1232
FROM BOOTCAMP
"Don't be too attached to your tools. They might slow you down. Eventually, they might keep you behind."
Dr. Bak Nguyen

1233
FROM TOUCHSTONE, LEVERAGING TODAY'S PSYCHOLOGICAL SMOG
"I say pressure because most of us are reacting, not pro acting."
Dr. Bak Nguyen

1234
FROM TOUCHSTONE, LEVERAGING TODAY'S PSYCHOLOGICAL SMOG
"Touchstones are triggers of the stress hormonal reaction. Knowing your way around them will shape your personality."
Dr. Bak Nguyen

1235
FROM TOUCHSTONE, LEVERAGING TODAY'S PSYCHOLOGICAL SMOG
"The more touchstones one keeps safe, the more handicaps one has."
Dr. Bak Nguyen

1236
FROM TOUCHSTONE, LEVERAGING TODAY'S PSYCHOLOGICAL SMOG
"The choice is very simple, are you looking for pride or for peace?"
Dr. Bak Nguyen

1237
FROM TOUCHSTONE, LEVERAGING TODAY'S PSYCHOLOGICAL SMOG
"Funny thing, in the dictionary, the word PRIDELESS does not exist. If I just made up that word, it is my contribution of the day to make the world a better place."
Dr. Bak Nguyen

1238
FROM TOUCHSTONE, LEVERAGING TODAY'S PSYCHOLOGICAL SMOG
"Kindness, patience and generosity."
Dr. Bak Nguyen

1239
FROM TOUCHSTONE, LEVERAGING TODAY'S PSYCHOLOGICAL SMOG
"Your journey will define who you are, until you are strong enough to become the journey itself."
Dr. Bak Nguyen

1240
FROM TOUCHSTONE, LEVERAGING TODAY'S PSYCHOLOGICAL SMOG
"Rise up to clarity and you will all see what is coming next."
Dr. Bak Nguyen

1241
FROM TOUCHSTONE, LEVERAGING TODAY'S PSYCHOLOGICAL SMOG
"I remain very hopeful since amongst all the possible stresses, my internet connexion was my main concern."
Dr. Bak Nguyen

1242
FROM TOUCHSTONE, LEVERAGING TODAY'S PSYCHOLOGICAL SMOG
"For as long as you are reacting,
you a late in the chain."
Dr. Bak Nguyen

1243
FROM ALPHA LADDERS VOLUME ONE
"We do with what we received.
We copy what we see."
Dr. Bak Nguyen

1244
FROM ALPHA LADDERS VOLUME ONE
"To each our own pace."
Dr. Bak Nguyen

1245
FROM ALPHA LADDERS VOLUME ONE
"There is no protection from openness.
You open yourself to vulnerability and
well as to enriching experiences."
Dr. Bak Nguyen

1246
FROM THE RISE OF THE UNICORN VOLUME TWO
"Sometimes, one must undo to learn to do again, better. and better meant differently."
Dr. Bak Nguyen

1247
FROM THE RISE OF THE UNICORN VOLUME TWO
"It was not Ambition that kept me going, it was Curiosity."
Dr. Bak Nguyen

1248
FROM THE RISE OF THE UNICORN VOLUME TWO
"I wrote and now, I could listen and react, not read again. I hate to read again. Except for sex and pleasure, I hate again."
Dr. Bak Nguyen

1249
FROM 1SELF
"To reinvent ourselves is to rewrite the future."
Dr. Bak Nguyen

1250
FROM 1SELF
"To write is to meditate, only with consequences."
Dr. Bak Nguyen

1251
FROM 1SELF
"This has become a number's game,
one with many words."
Dr. Bak Nguyen

1252
FROM 1SELF
"HUMILITY is the KEYSTONE to RELEVANCY."
Dr. Bak Nguyen

1253
FROM 1SELF
"By definition, all systems are moving. Their stability is coming from the continuation of their dynamic."
Dr. Bak Nguyen

1254
FROM 1SELF
"What is an asset today may become your biggest liability tomorrow."
Dr. Bak Nguyen

1255
FROM 1SELF
"It is never too late to reinvent ourselves, it never gets old either."
Dr. Bak Nguyen

1256
FROM 1SELF
"Your mindsets are the results of your experiences. They have an expiration date and a status of limitation, within the boundaries of that journey. There are so many other journeys ahead."
Dr. Bak Nguyen

1257
FROM 1SELF
"Rising isn't a moment, but an era."
Dr. Bak Nguyen

1258
FROM 1SELF
"Rising is a lonely path unless you are rising with and from compassion."
Dr. Bak Nguyen

1259
FROM ALPHA LADDERS VOLUME 2
"Knowledge may lead to power,
but without execution, knowledge is a burden
more than a blessing."
Dr. Bak Nguyen

1260
FROM ALPHA LADDERS VOLUME 2
"If you want a difference,
you need to think differently and to act as such."
Dr. Bak Nguyen

1261
FROM ALPHA LADDERS VOLUME 2
"Be open, be respectful, be flexible.
Look out for roots, for anchors, for attachments,
those will solve your doubts temporarily in exchange
for your freedom."
Dr. Bak Nguyen

1262
FROM THE BOOK OF LEGENDS VOLUME 3
"Nothing comes overnight. Some things will take
longer than others, but nothing is free, and sweat
does not mean that it is real."
Dr. Bak Nguyen

1263
FROM THE BOOK OF LEGENDS VOLUME 3
"The consequences of our choices
is the price of free will."
Dr. Bak Nguyen

1264
FROM THE BOOK OF LEGENDS VOLUME 3
"Nothing kills the music better than expectations."
Dr. Bak Nguyen

1265
FROM THE BOOK OF LEGENDS VOLUME 3
"The values will stand until the first win, and then,
he will have the chance to purge, sort and keep
only those he feels fit. In other words,
the minimum required!"
Dr. Bak Nguyen

1266
FROM MIRRORS
"To be ready, to listen, to be open."
Dr. Bak Nguyen

1267
FROM MIRRORS
"To have a mentor is to accept that we've reached the end of our mental mapping, yet."
Dr. Bak Nguyen

1268
FROM MIRRORS
"A weakness is a strength out of reach. We are either not strong or not smart enough to access it."
Dr. Bak Nguyen

1269
FROM MIRRORS
"From one level to the next, even gravity is relative."
Dr. Bak Nguyen

1270
FROM MIRRORS
"I know what I know and who I am; therefore I also know what I don't know and what I am not. now. No evolution nor growth is now out of reach."
Dr. Bak Nguyen

1271
FROM MIRRORS
"The longer the still, the thicker the ice."
Dr. Bak Nguyen

1272
FROM MIRRORS
"The more filters i try on, and lesser is the weight of habit from my past."
Dr. Bak Nguyen

1273
FROM MIRRORS
"To be aware is not to choose, to be aware is to be!"
Dr. Bak Nguyen

1274
FROM MIRRORS
"To tune in with the frequency of the universe, one must be in peace with oneself."
Dr. Bak Nguyen

1275
FROM MIRRORS
"Potential through actions,
that's how a mentor might notice you."
Dr. Bak Nguyen

1276
FROM THE CONFESSION OF AN OVERACHIEVER
"You can't be a squirrel and
hope to eat the lion's share."
Dr. Bak Nguyen

1277
FROM THE CONFESSION OF AN OVERACHIEVER
"The minute that you do a little more,
the average will be pulling you down."
Dr. Bak Nguyen

1278
FROM THE CONFESSION OF AN OVERACHIEVER
"The longer one stays at the edge of the cliff looking
down, the harder it will be to jump."
Dr. Bak Nguyen

1279
FROM THE CONFESSION OF AN OVERACHIEVER
"The blooming, just like everything else in the natural realm, does not last forever."
Dr. Bak Nguyen

1280
FROM THE CONFESSION OF AN OVERACHIEVER
"Motivation, that's often an environmental problem."
Dr. Bak Nguyen

1281
FROM THE CONFESSION OF AN OVERACHIEVER
"Don't try to control yourself. That's your cue to slow down and to regroup."
Dr. Bak Nguyen

1282
FROM TO OVERACHIEVER EVERYTHING BEING LAZY
"Looking back, there are pain and the insurance of no gain. Looking forward at least you have the hope of gain. What will counterbalance are fear and your perception of it."
Dr. Bak Nguyen

1283

FROM SHORTCUT VOLUME 1 - HEALING

"To write, I must feel first and then,
I dig to understand."

Dr. Bak Nguyen

This is **Shortcut volume 2, GROWTH**. Welcome to the Alphas.

Growth happens at the giving end.

Dr. BAK NGUYEN

PART 3
"LAZY"
by Dr. BAK NGUYEN

It was not easy growing. Growing as we are re-writing our DNA, culture, and education, fighting self-doubt and going against the odds made us stronger, unique. Only those who have done the trail will understand these words:

> "As we are singled out alone, left with doubt and insecurity, the growth happened, not by taking in more, but by giving more."
> Dr. Bak Nguyen

That is quote #2424. Growth happens at the giving end. As we are awakening, unsure of our identity and values, bringing in too much information will simply drown us with an ocean of choices and of possibilities. Without the proper sorting system, the intake of new information was worsening the problem.

Instead, what we needed was purpose, any purpose. To have a goal to serve and to move towards to, will help the purge of our burdens and the journey will strengthen our identity and confidence. That's how I came up with:

> *"Growth happens at the giving end,
> not the receiving one."*
> Dr. Bak Nguyen

A win at a time, you are growing into your destiny. What started as your story is slowly picking up pace and amplitude. You are now rising, not because you solved your identity crisis but because you started serving others. On the way, you found your values, identity, and confidence. To you, it was a liberation. To others, you are becoming a legend! And this is how your **RISE** is starting.

I am getting a little bit over myself… but you will have to excuse me, the excitement is just too great to silence. The **RISE** comes after **HEALING** and **GROWING**. We will cover this in the third volume of the series, with **CONFIDENCE** but how about a hack to the armoury?

If you are like me, you do not like waiting. Even if your strongest ally will be **CONFIDENCE** to keep rising and to walk your legend, here come the tools to leverage **CONFIDENCE**.

In the next part, let me share with you **THE POWER OF LAZINESS**.

> "Lazy does not mean that you don't have to do shit. It just means that you don't have to go through shit to gets things done."
> Dr. Bak Nguyen

I love this quote! It may lack finesse but the words and imagery are striking and clear. I spent half of my life conforming and pleasing. Then, I became a doctor. My function and power were to heal.

From healing teeth, I went on to heal fears, then confidences. For 20 years, I gave myself in the service of others, always putting their interests before mine. I gave but because I wasn't awake yet, I did not grow.

All of that changed the day one of my mentors told me that I have to forgive myself. That day, he opened a door in my soul, one that never closed again.

Then, I was running to catch up on the lost time. At the same time, I did not simply give up what I was presently doing, "Their interests before mine, remember?" So that kept me in line during my **AWAKENING, HEALING**, and **GROWTH**.

I was doing more and better as I kept piling up more challenges on top of my responsibilities. From a dentist to a CEO, from a CEO to a world record author, to a motivational speaker, and moving on to became an anchor of the Alphas.

How did I manage to do all of that? With the power and leverage of laziness. I simply had too much to do to care for the appearances, the sophistication, the rules, and the norms. I just did and reacted to what I was doing.

Being lazy allowed me to break all the frontiers I needed to pass. Actually, what it did was to erase procrastination completely. I had an idea, I saw a goal. I was too lazy to learn more, so I jumped right in, learning as I go.

Learning as you go, you quickly gain the sense of what is real and what is *BS*. Some will say that I have no respect for the art, the protocols, or the science. I was too lazy and too busy to even notice. I was respecting the goal, the people I am servicing, and the time that I was given.

This could have been a recipe for disaster: to do before to know. 3 mindsets kept me on track and in harmony with Society:

- To be Grateful
- To always put the interests of others before mine
- To understand the collaterals

I followed these rules instinctively, keeping these values from the legacy that I received. The rest faded away quickly as I moved forward.

Actually, I kept those because they ease the way, even when the horizon was unclear and stormy, they kept the light of hope up and to reduce the resistance ahead.

3 times within my awakening, I resisted the temptation of jumping into politics and to serve differently. My answer disappointed many. It even crushed my mentor's heart.

> "I was happy. I am lazy. Can you let me be?"
> Dr. Bak Nguyen

As this quote is #2425, it is also the exact words on which I departed ways with the man who awoken me. I never put my name on the ticket but I found other ways to serve and to make a difference.

I did so, not from a lack of concern or of engagement but because I was too lazy to fit in the process. I did not turn my back on leadership, I offered it my heart, which, thanks to the **POWER OF LAZINESS**, brought me to different horizons and perspectives.

You see, to me, only the results matter. The results and the smooth and quick way to arrive there. So no, I never meant to say *the result no matter the cost*. What I am saying is actually the opposite! Great for the result, and now, let do it at the smallest cost possible, in time and energy.

The **POWER OF LAZINESS** combined with the **POWER OF OPENNESS** propelled my rise. I was open to listen to the needs and desires of others. Then, I selected those I could help and I committed. My selection process was not based on what cause was better or more urgent. To me, that was judging. I simply stop doing that. For as long as it touches my heart, it was good enough to make it into my selection process.

If the goal was about them, the process was all about me. What can I do and how fast can I deliver? I learnt very quickly to acknowledge my talents and my limits. I did not spend much time trying to push my limits beyond, I simply bet on my talents.

> "It is not willpower that will erase your limits but the confidence coming from your wins."
> Dr. Bak Nguyen

That's quote #2426. A win after the next, I started to compile them. Of course, I failed a lot too. If winning boost my Confidence, losing fuelled my determination to win. And now you understand the **Cycle of Momentum**.

So what **LAZINESS** has to do with all of this? Well, Laziness is the spine of my speed. Laziness forced me to be smarter, more flexible, and to render. To be smarter and flexible are easy to get, but to render being lazy? Well, in every day's word, lazy isn't a compliment, it is a liability.

I bet on Laziness and I am in it to win. I could not afford to be proven wrong on that bet… I was simply too lazy to go back to the source to try something else. So I had no choice but to win, being lazy.

Because I was lazy, I stop judging. Because I was lazy, I sorted quickly the leverages from the liabilities. Because I was lazy, I did not care about labelling. Because I was lazy, I was not looking to be right, just to win. And I grew into a *kind tornado*, a *force of nature* (not my words, those are from my mentors).

World records after world records, recognitions, honours, and opportunities came one after the next at my doorsteps. I was not waiting for any of them. Some, I provoked, others were consequences of my actions and results. I just kept pushing forward, to my next win.

> "I am too lazy to stop and stare."
> Dr. Bak Nguyen

This is quote #2427. So you wanted to have secrets, to understand the power of my speed and momentum? You wanted to know the cheat and the hacks, here they are, the **MINDSET of LAZINESS**. These are the best of my leverage, the most useful in my armoury. Enjoy and make good use of them!

This is **Shortcut volume 2, GROWTH**. Welcome to the Alphas.

Growth happens at the giving end
Dr. BAK NGUYEN

PART 4
"32 LAZY QUOTES"
by Dr. BAK NGUYEN

2381
FROM THE BOOK OF LEGENDS, VOLUME 1
"I am lazy since I've reached harmony..."
Dr. Bak Nguyen

2382
FROM HOW TO WRITE A BOOK IN 30 DAYS
"My laziness is often sourced from my success."
Dr. Bak Nguyen

2383
FROM POWER, EMOTIONAL INTELLIGENCE
"I am lazy. What was supposed to be a liability turned out to be a blessing, one I learnt to leverage on."
Dr. Bak Nguyen

2384
FROM MASTERMIND
"4 hours for 15% versus 1 hour for 85%, the deal is pretty clear to me."
Dr. Bak Nguyen

2385
FROM MASTERMIND
"Only care about the things you can change. The rest are extra burdens that you don't need."
Dr. Bak Nguyen

2386
FROM THE MODERN WOMAN
"I grew twice, but only pay the price once.
That's the great deal of being lazy!"
Dr. Bak Nguyen

2387
FROM TOUCHSTONE, LEVERAGING TODAY'S PSYCHOLOGICAL SMOG
"I am too lazy to spend my life running from something. I prefer to run towards that something. It is the shorter way."
Dr. Bak Nguyen

2388
FROM TOUCHSTONE, LEVERAGING TODAY'S PSYCHOLOGICAL SMOG
"I am too lazy to have projects
laying around in my mind."
Dr. Bak Nguyen

2389
FROM ALPHA LADDERS VOLUME ONE
"I am just a lazy guy looking for fun."
Dr. Bak Nguyen

2390
FROM THE CONFESSION OF AN OVERACHIEVER
"If you are looking to be lazy, learn to leverage!"
Dr. Bak Nguyen

2391
FROM THE CONFESSION OF AN OVERACHIEVER
"I study to be lazy. I choose what I study to be smarter."
Dr. Bak Nguyen

2392
FROM THE CONFESSION OF AN OVERACHIEVER
"Study the systems, those are the keys to leverage your laziness."
Dr. Bak Nguyen

2393
FROM THE CONFESSION OF AN OVERACHIEVER
"Don't crave yourself, feed yourself as much as possible."
Dr. Bak Nguyen

2394
FROM TO OVERACHIEVER EVERYTHING BEING LAZY
"And so, busy and lazy became one."
Dr. Bak Nguyen

2395
FROM TO OVERACHIEVER EVERYTHING BEING LAZY
"To ease in, anywhere and in anything, is the most difficult task since we need motivation and fighting against resistance without any velocity."
Dr. Bak Nguyen

2396
FROM TO OVERACHIEVER EVERYTHING BEING LAZY
"Motivation is something you need to begin. Once in action, velocity and dedication will keep you up, not motivation."
Dr. Bak Nguyen

2397
FROM TO OVERACHIEVER EVERYTHING BEING LAZY
"To ease in is the best approach then to have to check-in. and once in, do not check-out."
Dr. Bak Nguyen

2398
FROM TO OVERACHIEVER EVERYTHING BEING LAZY
"Trust me, when you stand right in the middle of the storm, it is calm and simple."
Dr. Bak Nguyen

2399
FROM TO OVERACHIEVER EVERYTHING BEING LAZY
"Personally, I hate to come back to my footsteps,
so I move forward."
Dr. Bak Nguyen

2400
FROM TO OVERACHIEVER EVERYTHING BEING LAZY
"Your head and your sight dictate your trajectory.
Keep your head up."
Dr. Bak Nguyen

2401
FROM TO OVERACHIEVER EVERYTHING BEING LAZY
"At an individual level, you might find many variances.
Group the variances and you will define trends."
Dr. Bak Nguyen

2402
FROM TO OVERACHIEVER EVERYTHING BEING LAZY
"Whatever your reasons, never stand in the way
of a stampede, you might face the
worse part of the storm."
Dr. Bak Nguyen

2403

FROM TO OVERACHIEVER EVERYTHING BEING LAZY
"Jumping from holes to holes,
you will be travelling mountains."
Dr. Bak Nguyen

2404
FROM TO OVERACHIEVER EVERYTHING BEING LAZY
"Stop choosing one or the other. Be lazy and take them both! Choosing can be exhausting!"
Dr. Bak Nguyen

2405
FROM TO OVERACHIEVER EVERYTHING BEING LAZY
"There is no free money in life. There is easier and harder money though."
Dr. Bak Nguyen

2406
FROM TO OVERACHIEVER EVERYTHING BEING LAZY
"Study the systems to evolve.
The better you understand the system,
the less you will have to work."
Dr. Bak Nguyen

2407
FROM TO OVERACHIEVER EVERYTHING BEING LAZY
"You wanted to be lazy and to overachieve,
be the first to react and before having
no more choice, lead the trend!"
Dr. Bak Nguyen

2408
FROM TO OVERACHIEVER EVERYTHING BEING LAZY
"Because I am lazy, I do not procrastinate."
Dr. Bak Nguyen

2409
FROM TO OVERACHIEVER EVERYTHING BEING LAZY
"A fact is a fact, negative or positive,
it is up to you to decide."
Dr. Bak Nguyen

2410
FROM TO OVERACHIEVER EVERYTHING BEING LAZY
"Be lazy enough to throw procrastination away."
Dr. Bak Nguyen

2411
FROM TO OVERACHIEVER EVERYTHING BEING LAZY

"Lazy and easy, I love those words. with the right mindset, they will come with wins too!"

Dr. Bak Nguyen

2412
FROM TO OVERACHIEVER EVERYTHING BEING LAZY

"To grow without resistance is the fastest way to grow, even if the journey is a never-ending one."

Dr. Bak Nguyen

This is **Shortcut volume 2, GROWTH**. Welcome to the Alphas.

Growth happens at the giving end.

Dr. BAK NGUYEN

PART 5
"THE POWER OF QUOTES"
by Dr. BAK NGUYEN

What a journey! What started as a cheat grew to become one of my greatest hacks of all time, to revive reading, adapting it with the trends of the day. Covering the second chapter of the **POWER OF QUOTES**, here I am sharing with you how started to write quotes.

Back in my days in college, I read a lot for leisure. What a nerd some might say. Actually, I was reading to escape from the boredom of class, sciences, and academia. I read about History, about conquests, about myths and legends.

The first quote that ever came to me was in French as I was taking the subway home:

"Vivre un rêve, c'est là le rêve d'une vie."
Dr. Bak Nguyen

"To live a dream is the dream of a lifetime." That just appeared in my mind as I was observing people going on with their lives. That was 25 years ago. I never gave much thought or effort into finding more quotes.

Much later in life, as I started preparing for my first appearance on stage, I resumed using of quotes as titles, a shocking and provocative title to appeal to my audience. I started with a bold affirmation and spent the rest of the speech explaining myself. That's how quotes became my signature.

As I am very lazy, I did not stop at the title. I realized that every time that I was making an affirmation, it was better understood in the form of a quote. Edited and designed as such, it took fewer words to express myself. Moreover, it gave me a tool to pace my texts and speeches.

So I wrote quotes as I was breathing my words and thoughts, from one chapter to the next. Writing quotes also gave me another edge. As I am signing each of my quotes, it gave me the small satisfaction of a win before the final win of completing the book.

From one small win to the next, my body was empowered to propel itself further and further. One paragraph at a time, one quote after the next, words became chapters and chapters wrote books at a world record pace. In a word, I leveraged.

I started the use of quotes because I was lazy. Then, I was aware and open to the ripple effect and surfed the waves.

> "From laziness to surf the wins with the power of hormones and of satisfaction, I rode my legend."
> Dr. Bak Nguyen

And that is the 2428th quote! Here are 8 in-depth coverages of these 77 famous quotes that I cherish. I will explain and share with you shortly their story, 8 at a time, respecting the number of the Dragon. May they inspire you and find their use in the palm of your hands.

FAMOUS QUOTE 1

> 0002
> FROM SYMPHONY OF SKILLS
> "Sharing is the way to grow."
> Dr. Bak Nguyen

That was amongst my first quotes. I was still new to the form and came up with this one very instinctively. As I was writing my first book, not thinking that it was a book but a series of Ted Talks, I really felt my heart and influence growing as I was addressing an audience, you.

As you are making me feeling bigger and important, I needed a way to keep your attention and interest. What better way to do that but to empowering you to your dreams and desires. As a doctor, I spent the first half of my career treating people's pains and fears. Then, as I found my strength, I went on to empower their desire and confidence as a cosmetic surgeon. Never have I connected more with my patients.

So I grew as a surgeon, empowering the desires and needs of those under my care. It was a logical step for me to use empowerment to embrace the stage. So I did, I empowered you, sharing freely my journey, wins and losses, hoping to inspire you.

Doing anything of worth, the most difficult part is the beginning when you are breaking from your shell. People hate that, they hate to see one of their peers rise above the average, above them. I was breaking from my shell and from the ranks. I was sharing my story, the only things I could talk about with insurance and confidence. I shared only what I did and felt, nothing more. I hate opinions, so I refrain myself from giving you mine.

They shout to my face that I was bragging, that they too have a story. The difference is that I was willing to share mine as they stood still with their arms crossed over their chest. *They chipped another piece of their soul judging me.* Meanwhile, I open my heart and connect with you, so many of you, sharing with you a piece of my soul, of my life. In return, you gave me your love and respect.

Before I knew it, I was talking to people that I never met, never even talked to. People knew me as a familiar face when I had no idea who they were. As I was walking the streets of downtown, before COVID and the mask, I got smiles and respectful greetings. Some even went to me to shake my hand and ask for a picture. What I did touch them. They thanked me for sharing and to have inspired them.

That was more than I bargained for. I was sharing and felt good doing so. I did so, keeping the interests of my audience at heart. Well, I open my heart and they gave me theirs. What do you think happened next? I doubled down and shared more and at an even greater pace! Empowerment will go a long, long way!

FAMOUS QUOTE 2

0005
FROM PROFESSION HEALTH
"Mine was, forgive yourself."
Dr. Bak Nguyen

Those are the words of Dr. Mohamed Behkhalifa, one of my mentors and coach. With that single phrase, he opened a door in my soul that opened the possibility of Growth. As a doctor, I gave and gave each day, day after day. I grew, but very slowly and with baby steps.

Now, we all know that "Growth happens at the giving end." I was giving but not growing because I was not awaken, not aware. As Dr. Benkhalifa removed the denial and the burden of guilt off of my heart, I finally stood tall.

There, I could see life from a different angle, not aimed at my *belly button* anymore. I became available. Because I forgave myself, I forgot my *belly button*. Standing tall, I found Confidence and was finally open and available to take in more of life.

Denial and guilt will crush a soul much more than rejection and failure ever will. If my mom gave me birth,

Dr. Benkhalifa gave me back my wings that day, telling me to forgive myself.

Anchors and regrets are all from the past. To live is to look to the future. To be selfless is not just to look beyond your *belly button*. The only way to do that is to stand tall and to look up, not down. Forgive yourself and feel the freedom and power coming with them.

FAMOUS QUOTE 3

0007
FROM INDUSTRIES' DISRUPTORS
"If I have changed the world from a dental chair, you are all in a better position than I am to change the world."
Dr. Bak Nguyen

Empowerment, this is all about empowerment. Actually, my whole rise is about empowerment, empowering you to be your best. As I started rising, now lighter with the **POWER OF FORGIVENESS**, I started sharing in books and conferences. At my first appearance on stage, this one came to my mouth as a surprise.

I was easing into my new role as a motivational speaker. Caught between two veteran speakers, great and with much charisma, I was nervous. But that all fade away as I focused on you, the audience, instead of on myself. So I had fun sharing on stage, even talking a tongue in which I had to think twice about each of my words and pronunciation.

Changing the world from a dental chair became my signature. It was not planned nor scripted, it just came as I was addressing the audience. From the bottom of my heart, I really meant each of these words. If I am standing there, on stage, explaining how I made a difference as a dentist, stuck within so many norms and regulations, all of you are in a much better position than I am to change the world. The crowd was moved and elevated in ovation.

Years later, I cross paths with some of the people who were in the audience that day. Years later, they are still coming to me and thanking me for the inspiration, years later. That's empowerment! Both ways!

So yes, if I am changing the world from a dental chair, imagine what you can do!

FAMOUS QUOTE 4

0019
FROM MOMENTUM TRANSFER
"On thin ice, speed up, that's how you will eventually learn to fly!"
Dr. Bak Nguyen

This one came up much later in my career as a writer and motivational speaker. It really means literally what it sounds. People have an old saying that one has to crawl first before one can walk and run. Well, that is one anchor that will kill many of you.

If you are walking on solid ground, that might be true. Actually, it is only true as one needs steps and small increments to advance. That's ok but that's not a truth, just a reality to some.

Now, put that in perspective. We are living and the world is spinning, faster and faster. Live is changing faster and faster. Nothing is solid ground. Maybe, nothing was ever solid. This is a fact hard to ignore. With that in mind, what we consider solid is only the surface, just like ice, thin ice.

Walking on ice, what is safer? To crawl, to walk, or to run? None of the above. On ice, you want to surf, leaving as little resistance as possible. And that is on ice, where the surface is frozen and consider solid. Most of life is streaming like a river. And the opportunities lay in these rivers and oceans.

So what do you do? Do you want to learn to crawl to learn to walk and eventually, learn to run? You did all of that on solid ground (which is an illusion and where life and opportunities lack). Learn to run to learn to surf as soon as possible. Master surfing and soon enough, you will be flying before you know!

The key to this quote is speed. Do not procrastinate, do. As you do, repeat the process faster and faster to change your inertia into energy and momentum. From there, the rules aren't the same…

FAMOUS QUOTE 5

0023
FROM HYBRID
"A weakness is a strength out of reach."
Dr. Bak Nguyen

Nothing is set in stone. Every time you are judging, you a chipping away a piece of your soul. This is what a weakness is, ignorance and labelling. What is an asset today can be a liability tomorrow. Your medals, even if you got as many as Olympic swimmer Micheal Phelps, will you wear them to your next contest?

The same applies to your failures. Live the moment, take in the lessons and move on, good or bad. What today seems to be a distraction and a liability is simply the realization that you are not ready yet to embrace it. You may never be ready and that's fine too. But refrain yourself to discard it completely, you may be cutting yourself from your best leverage.

Personally, I am not aiming at my weaknesses. I bet on my strengths and jump from challenge to challenge. After I stop judging, I also stop judging myself. I do not have weakness or liability anymore. I just look at everything that I am, that I have as a possibility. If I can leverage it to move forward, I will. If not, I move on until next time.

So I did with love, friendship, family, friends, positions, projects, ideas, and ambitions. Each has their place and time. I made my peace with that.

2429
FROM SHORTCUT 2, GROWTH
"To find harmony and synergy,
it is all about timing, not labelling."
Dr. Bak Nguyen

FAMOUS QUOTE 6

0025
FROM REBOOT, TO GROW FROM MIDLIFE CRISIS
"Don't stop the flow of a river unless
you are ready to clean up the flood."
Dr. Bak Nguyen

This one should be obvious and yet, this is what Society sets us up against. We are born powerful and free. By shaping us into a member of collectivity, it muted most of our power and potential in exchange for stability.

Being grateful, I like to think that it did so to prepare us to be ready for our powers. Younger, I might not have the wisdom to control such power nor to yield it for the best of society. They created a nurturing period in which, just like going to school, through the ranks, I learnt to master patience and discipline.

In truth, it is all about control. The design was to fade away the power and aspirations to keep control for as long as possible. With age, we all fade in energy… until willpower and determination kick in. But once we are awake, that dam that Society created to contain us will not last long.

Who would like to stand at the feet of a breaking dam? Well, this is what Society set us up to. We stand in the ways of those we love and neighbour, telling them to come down to Earth, to tell them to crawl, and to communicate our fears and limitations in the name of love and protection.

2430
FROM SHORTCUT 2, GROWTH
"Fear is a virus, we should fight it
instead of spreading it around."
Dr. Bak Nguyen

But once more, most of Society is not looking to empower but to keep under control, under management. So fear becomes a leverage rather than a virus to kill. More than once, I told you that the power contained within our heart and body is great. Well, accessing fear will unleash that kind of power.

Now imagine having access to the same kind of power but releasing it with purpose and ambition instead of fear. To use Greed to pull, instead of Fear to push. And why should we do so? Pulling, we are pulling up, while pushing, well, that can go both ways... Why take the chance of ever pushing down?

I learnt to always pull. Tension is much safer than pressure as it comes to empowerment. And once empower, we are our own river full of life and energy. One can guide the flow. Trying to control it, one must be much greater to contain such energy... until he or she becomes the dam that stops the **flow of life**.

This goes as you are in a position of power, looking to guide the others. Holding too tight to control and you are the pressure pushing them to react. Empower them with kindness and you are pulling them to elevate themselves and you with them. Either way, be ready to surf the waves of energy. Thinking that you can control and absorb all of it might be your last mistake. And where is the fun in that anyway?

FAMOUS QUOTE 7

0030
FROM THE BOOK OF LEGENDS, VOLUME 1
"Humility is the ability to recognize and
to respect what we are, and stop pretending
to be what we are not."
Dr. Bak Nguyen

In **HEALING**, we've learnt to recognize denial and to acknowledge what is and what is not. Then, it was about finding our place in Life. The only way to find our rightful place, contrary to common beliefs, is not by grabbing, fighting, and stealing our way through life. No, no one will present us with our destiny on a plate. Destiny is made to be walked.

Even if nothing is free, **GROWING** by giving will help us understand our powers and talents. It will nurture our Confidence and prepare us for what is coming next. **RISING** is to do something of worth with all these powers flooding in our veins.

This is the right wording and order. Humility is to accept what we are and to see who we are not. Humility is the key to **HEALING** since one has to accept who he is and who he is not, a pre-requirement to **GROWING** since one has to learn and grow with confidence:

2431
FROM SHORTCUT 2, GROWTH
"Humility is the only way to Confidence
without the liability of Pride."
Dr. Bak Nguyen

And humility is the cornerstone of **RISING** without resistance.

One does not have to be perfect to make a difference in the world
One must be Confident to lead a force of change
One must empower the others in order to keep rising without resistance

Those are the keys to success
This is the power of Humility.

So forget what they taught you about humility. Humility is not to lower your head, neglecting who you are, and asking them for permission. Humility is an internal process, one keeping Pride in check.

2431
FROM SHORTCUT 2, GROWTH
"Only once humble, can one be available to truly give and grow."
Dr. Bak Nguyen

FAMOUS QUOTE 8

0037
FROM HOW TO WRITE A BOOK IN 30 DAYS
"To keep Momentum, aim for the next win, as little as it might be."
Dr. Bak Nguyen

If there is an ultimate quote about **HOW TO BUILD CONFIDENCE**, this one is first on the list. You can be born confident or have burdened yourself with doubt, move forward to your next win and everything will fall in place.

Doubt and Confidence can not co-exist. Once Confident, you know the way, you feel the way. You might be wrong, but as you will survive your journey, you will eventually know the way.

And since everything is moving and changing, there is no right way. What was right this time may be wrong by the next. What you learnt was to trust your instincts and to keep moving without second-guessing yourself at each turn.

When you stop and think about it, what good reason do we have to doubt ourselves? Some might say that it will keep our Pride in check. Well, they are as right as to say that to make sure that a child will learn to crawl, break his legs first! Can you see the non-sense in that? Well, keep doubting and this is what you are doing to yourself, breaking your spirit!

To keep Pride in check, you need to understand the **POWER OF HUMILITY**, which is the key to real Confidence and to each and every win you will ever have. Try to rise without the **POWER OF HUMILITY** and be prepared to meet a lot of resistance on your way.

Personally, I am too lazy to face resistance.

This is **Shortcut volume 2, GROWTH**. Welcome to the Alphas.

Growth happens at the giving end.

Dr. BAK NGUYEN

PART 6
"FAMOUS QUOTES"
by Dr. BAK NGUYEN

0001
FROM SYMPHONY OF SKILLS
"The pain of the problem has to be greater than the pain of change."
Dr. Bak Nguyen

0002
FROM SYMPHONY OF SKILLS
"Sharing is the way to grow."
Dr. Bak Nguyen

0003
FROM LEADERSHIP, PANDORA'S BOX
"One's legend can only begin the day one's Quest of Identity is over."
Dr. Bak Nguyen

0004
FROM IDENTITY, ANTHOLOGY OF QUESTS
"Gratitude is the only past with a future."
Dr. Bak Nguyen

0005
FROM PROFESSION HEALTH
"Mine was, forgive yourself."
Dr. Bak Nguyen

0006
FROM INDUSTRIES' DISRUPTORS
"To walk on thin ice is a dangerous game.
To run is safer. To surf is the easiest."
Dr. Bak Nguyen

0007
FROM INDUSTRIES' DISRUPTORS
"If I have changed the world from a dental chair,
you are all in a better position than I am
to change the world."
Dr. Bak Nguyen

0008
FROM INDUSTRIES' DISRUPTORS
"The day you are fighting to raise the average instead
of beating it, that day, you've joined the leadership."
Dr. Bak Nguyen

0009
FROM INDUSTRIES' DISRUPTORS
"At the end of the day, business is communication."
Dr. Bak Nguyen

0010
FROM INDUSTRIES' DISRUPTORS
"Make leverage of each of your liabilities, and you will always be moving forward."
Dr. Bak Nguyen

0011
FROM INDUSTRIES' DISRUPTORS
"I believe in myself and I do it for God, not the other way around."
Dr. Bak Nguyen

0012
FROM INDUSTRIES' DISRUPTORS
"Always choose the path of least resistance."
Dr. Bak Nguyen

0013
FROM INDUSTRIES' DISRUPTORS
"Be mindful of the consequences."
Dr. Bak Nguyen

0014
FROM CHANGING THE WORLD FROM A DENTAL CHAIR
"Hammering air three times over and it will become steel."
Dr. Bak Nguyen

0015
FROM CHANGING THE WORLD FROM A DENTAL CHAIR
"Mdex, for joy for life."
Dr. Bak Nguyen

0016
FROM CHANGING THE WORLD FROM A DENTAL CHAIR
"Confidence is sexy."
Dr. Bak Nguyen

0017
FROM CHANGING THE WORLD FROM A DENTAL CHAIR
"Make it happen!"
Dr. Bak Nguyen

0018
FROM THE POWER BEHIND THE ALPHA
"Humility is to know what you are and to recognize what you are not."
Dr. Bak Nguyen

0019
FROM MOMENTUM TRANSFER
"On thin ice, speed up, that's how you will eventually learn to fly!"
Dr. Bak Nguyen

0020
FROM MOMENTUM TRANSFER
"Control with wisdom is called influence."
Dr. Bak Nguyen

0021
FROM MOMENTUM TRANSFER
"To stabilize a momentum, speed up!"
Dr. Bak Nguyen

0022
FROM HYBRID
"Chords and patterns are the themes of the Universe."
Dr. Bak Nguyen

0023
FROM HYBRID
"A weakness is a strength out of reach."
Dr. Bak Nguyen

0024
FROM HYBRID
"Look for your next immediate win."
Dr. Bak Nguyen

0025
FROM REBOOT, TO GROW FROM MIDLIFE CRISIS
"Don't stop the flow of a river unless you are ready to clean up the flood."
Dr. Bak Nguyen

0026
FROM LEVERAGE COMMUNICATION INTO SUCCESS
"Find your worth in the service of others."
Dr. Bak Nguyen

0027
FROM LEVERAGE COMMUNICATION INTO SUCCESS
"Humility is not the denial of oneself but the acceptance of one true nature."
Dr. Bak Nguyen

0028
FROM THE BOOK OF LEGENDS, VOLUME 1
"We are all born little, as a chicken heart. If we keep an open mind, we will grow into a lion heart. Some will choose to be close-minded and will remain small."
Dr. Bak Nguyen

0029
FROM THE BOOK OF LEGENDS, VOLUME 1
"To have an open mind is step one.
To keep growing, one needs an open heart."
Dr. Bak Nguyen

0030
FROM THE BOOK OF LEGENDS, VOLUME 1
"Humility is the ability to recognize and to respect what we are, and stop pretending to be what we are not."
Dr. Bak Nguyen

0031
FROM SELFMADE
"Good things start to happen when you say yes!"
Dr. Bak Nguyen

0032
FROM SELFMADE
"Knowledge is the ground of the past.
Hope and Dreams are the air of the future."
Dr. Bak Nguyen

0033
FROM SELFMADE
"My deepest fear is to show up before God and not have enough to show for."
Dr. Bak Nguyen

0034
FROM THE RISE OF THE UNICORN
"To make the world a better place."
Dr. Bak Nguyen

0035
FROM THE RISE OF THE UNICORN
"A Momentum is when it is easier to keep moving than to stop."
Dr. Bak Nguyen

0036
FROM CHAMPION MINDSET
"I was open, and I bet on myself."
Dr. Bak Nguyen

0037
FROM HOW TO WRITE A BOOK IN 30 DAYS
"To keep Momentum, aim for the next win, as little as it might be."
Dr. Bak Nguyen

0038
FROM HOW TO WRITE A BOOK IN 30 DAYS
"A quote is a truth from another life, from a past legacy."
Dr. Bak Nguyen

0039
FROM HOW TO WRITE A BOOK IN 30 DAYS
"The fewer the words, the better."
Dr. Bak Nguyen

0040
FROM POWER, EMOTIONAL INTELLIGENCE
"Align your emotions and your ambitions to be whole, to be unstoppable."
Dr. Bak Nguyen

0041
FROM POWER, EMOTIONAL INTELLIGENCE
"I believe in myself, and I do it for God, not the other way around."
Dr. Bak Nguyen

0042
FROM BRANDING
"I kept the "Dr." on to remind me to always put your interests before mine."
Dr. Bak Nguyen

0043
FROM BRANDING
"Arrogance is not the bragging of our knowledge, but rather the denial of our ignorance."
Dr. Bak Nguyen

0044
FROM HORIZON VOLUME ONE
"I treat people, not teeth."
Dr. Bak Nguyen

0045
FROM THE POWER OF YES, VOLUME 1
"Writing books allowed me to evolve at the speed of my thoughts."
Dr. Bak Nguyen

0046
FROM THE POWER OF YES, VOLUME 1
"Speed is my power. Momentum, my expression."
Dr. Bak Nguyen

0047
FROM THE POWER OF YES VOLUME 3
"We do not need to choose, only to prioritize."
Dr. Bak Nguyen

0048
FROM HOW TO NOT FAIL AS A DENTIST
"Changing the world from a dental chair."
Dr. Bak Nguyen

0049
FROM HOW TO NOT FAIL AS A DENTIST
"I am not giving up, I am simply wising up!"

Dr. Bak Nguyen

0050
FROM HOW TO NOT FAIL AS A DENTIST
"With your money, do not trust anyone but yourself."

Dr. Bak Nguyen

0051
FROM HUMILITY FOR SUCCESS
"Reading will be cool again!"

Dr. Bak Nguyen

0052
FROM HUMILITY FOR SUCCESS
"Until it is done, it is air, good air but only air."

Dr. Bak Nguyen

0053
FROM MASTERMIND
"You can cheat, legally, by learning about shortcuts and leveraging."

Dr. Bak Nguyen

0054
FROM PLAYBOOK INTRODUCTION VOLUME 1
"Nothing will last forever, and nothing is free."
Dr. Bak Nguyen

0055
FROM PLAYBOOK INTRODUCTION VOLUME 2
"Be careful since doubts is a pet
that you are feeding."
Dr. Bak Nguyen

0056
FROM PLAYBOOK INTRODUCTION VOLUME 2
"Reach for your next win as soon as possible,
and build on it!"
Dr. Bak Nguyen

0057
FROM AMONGST THE ALPHAS, VOLUME 2
"Be bold, confident, and humble."
Dr. Bak Nguyen

0058
FROM AMONGST THE ALPHAS, VOLUME 2
"Growth happens at the giving end,
not the receiving one."
Dr. Bak Nguyen

0059
FROM SUCCESS IS A CHOICE
"Be bold, be flexible, act fast and stay humble."
Dr. Bak Nguyen

0060
FROM SUCCESS IS A CHOICE
"To succeed, be flexible."
Dr. Bak Nguyen

0061
FROM 90 DAYS CHALLENGE
"In times of crisis, one has to reinvent oneself."
Dr. Bak Nguyen

0062
FROM RISING
"To matter, serve."
Dr. Bak Nguyen

0063
FROM RISING
"There is no free money."
Dr. Bak Nguyen

0064
FROM AFTERMATH
"For the first time of our lifetime, all the interests of the world are aligned."
Dr. Bak Nguyen

0065
FROM AFTERMATH
"In times of crisis, it is the perfect opportunity to reinvent who we are."
Dr. Bak Nguyen

0066
FROM AFTERMATH
"Yes, we can have it all!"
Dr. Bak Nguyen

0067
FROM TORNADO
"History will say that to celebrate one world record, we scored two more!"
Dr. Bak Nguyen

0068
FROM TORNADO
"The only way to keep overdelivering is playing, all-in!"
Dr. Bak Nguyen

0069
FROM TORNADO
"Dream and the means will come."
Dr. Bak Nguyen

0070
FROM ALPHA LADDERS VOLUME ONE
"All good things start with a YES."
Dr. Bak Nguyen

0071
FROM ALPHA LADDERS VOLUME 2
"Growth occurs at the giving end, always."
Dr. Bak Nguyen

0072
FROM THE CONFESSION OF AN OVERACHIEVER
"Being lazy doesn't mean that you don't have to do shit, it means that you don't have to go through shit to get things done."
Dr. Bak Nguyen

0073
FROM TO OVERACHIEVER EVERYTHING BEING LAZY
"Arrogance is not the recognition of who we are but the denial of what we are not."
Dr. Bak Nguyen

0074
FROM TO OVERACHIEVER EVERYTHING BEING LAZY
"You call me doctor to remind me to always put your needs before mine."

Dr. Bak Nguyen

0075
FROM TO OVERACHIEVER EVERYTHING BEING LAZY
"Nowadays, influence is power without liability."

Dr. Bak Nguyen

0076
FROM TO OVERACHIEVER EVERYTHING BEING LAZY
"I told you that everything in life is a trade. Be careful of what you are trading."

Dr. Bak Nguyen

0077
FROM SHORTCUT VOLUME 1 - HEALING
"Fear is a disease and it must be treated like one."

Dr. Bak Nguyen

This is **Shortcut volume 2, GROWTH**. Welcome to the Alphas.

Growth happens at the giving end

Dr. BAK NGUYEN

CONCLUSION
by Dr. BAK NGUYEN

What a journey. I congratulate you all to have initiated your personal journey, your Quest of Identity. In **SHORTCUT VOLUME 1**, you awoke and start your healing.

> "Yes, we all need healing, somehow."
> Dr. Bak Nguyen

Then, in this volume, **SHORTCUT VOLUME 2**, you continued your journey growing while healing. It is a personal and long process. Some will take more time than others, some will just pass as if it was a breeze. That is all okay, we each have our pace and our story to walk.

Growing while sorting each of our values and beliefs is not an easy thing, not to anyone. It is a journey that everyone will have to walk, sooner or later. It is one that you will have to do alone, that's the essence of the Quest of Identity. But as soon as you found your core and heart, you will also find new allies.

If everyone needs healing, well, sooner or later, everyone will grow. The only questions are **WHEN**, **HOW**, and **HOW MUCH**, you will grow. This is why it is so important to understand the steps ahead of each of us, looking for our name, looking for success, looking for freedom, looking for happiness.

This is a universal quest. That said, if the quest is universal, not everyone will touch their dreams and their Destiny. This one is a matter of choices and of circumstances.

> "Growing happens at the giving end."
> Dr. Bak Nguyen

HEALING was the first step. **GROWING** followed closely. **RISING** is the next stage. The next 4 volumes of the **SHORTCUT** series are dedicated to **RISING**. **LEADERSHIP**, **CONFIDENCE**, **SUCCESS**, and **POWER** are the next themes of **SHORTCUT**.

As you can now see clearly, there are many ways to rise, to be successful, to be happy. But it all started with the healing process complete and the growth from giving. What to heal from, that we inherited and did not choose. What and how to give, that is entirely our choice. No matter what and how you are giving, you will be growing (once you have awakened).

And then, how you will rise will depend on your choices and determination to see your choices through. Will that be **SUCCESS**, will that be **HAPPINESS**, will that be **LEADERSHIP** or **POWER**? Or will it be a combination of them? Why not all of them?

That is for you to choose and for you to make into your reality. From your rise, you will be walking your Destiny. Finding your name and your worth was just the beginning of your journey.

> "One's legend can only begin the day one's Quest of Identity is over."
> Dr. Bak Nguyen

Well, this is where your personal journey ends, now that you are out of your Quest of Identity. You've healed and you've grown. To find your worth is next, as you will be rising.

If that journey will be retold as a legend, it will depend on how you will walk it and how many people you will have helped and inspired on your way. Growth should be a mean to a bigger end. I grew exponentially looking to share. This is a fact, I did more within my last 4 years than in the first 40. How did that happen?

> "Growth became exponential as it became
> a side effect of my quests."
> Dr. Bak Nguyen

The more I talked, the more I walked
The words became books
And the books became quotes

I gained momentum
Moving from one win to the next
Speed, Flexibility, and Compassion
Contribute to my rise
One with lesser resistance,
Doing the impossible

Heal and make peace with your past
Grow as you are looking to serve
More than you seek answers

You do not possess the right questions
But the answers are always right
Make sense of them
And leverage your story
Into your Destiny.

Your Destiny, this is what it is all about, you! Don't shy away from the question, only you can answer that question. Be humble and you will rise. But no one can rise without confidence, caring only doubt in his or her heart.

Know that the key to real confidence is humility. Get your wording right and start what you always felt inside, what you know to be right, to be true. Your emotions will never lie. Learn to listen to them and they will become your best allies.

You are now out of your Quest of Identity. You may have never noticed the transition, but you are now starting your rise. Find your worth, find your powers and walk your Destiny.

I wish you luck and fortune, but right before, I gave you my best tools to leverage with, the **LAZY mindsets**. Keep those close to your heart and mind.

Once you have set your goals, the **LAZY mindsets** will empower you to find ease on your journey, maybe assist you in creating your momentum. I can't wait to read about you and your legend!

This is **Shortcut volume 2, GROWTH**. Welcome to the Alphas.

Growth happens at the giving end.

Dr. BAK NGUYEN

ANNEX
GLOSSARY OF Dr. BAK's LIBRARY

1

1SELF -080

REINVENT YOURSELF FROM ANY CRISIS
BY Dr. BAK NGUYEN

In 1SELF is about to reinvent yourself to rise from any crisis. Written in the midst of the COVID war, now more than ever, we need hope and the know-how to bridge the future. More than just the journey of Dr. Bak, this time, Dr. Bak is sharing his journey with mentors and people who built part of the world as we know it. Interviewed in this book, CHRISTIAN TRUDEAU, former CEO and FOUNDER of BCE EMERGIS (BELL CANADA), he also digitalized the Montreal Stock Exchange.RON KLEIN, American Innovator, inventor of the magnetic stripe of the credit card, of MLS (Multi-listing services) and the man who digitalized WALL STREET bonds markets.ANDRE CHATELAIN, former first vice-president of the MOVEMENT DES JARDINS. Dr. JEAN DE SERRES, former CEO of HEMA QUEBEC. These men created billions in values and have changed our lives, even without us knowing. They all come together to share their experiences and knowledge to empower each and everyone to emerge stronger from this crisis, from any crisis.

AFTERMATH -063
BUSINESS AFTER THE GREAT PAUSE
BY Dr. BAK NGUYEN & Dr. ERIC LACOSTE

In AFTERMATH, Dr. Bak joins forces with Community leader and philanthrope Dr. Eric Lacoste. Two powerful minds and forces of nature in the reaction to the worst economic meltdown in modern times. We are all victims of the CORONA virus. Both just like humans have learned to adapt to survive, so is our economy. Most business structures and management philosophies are inherited from the age of industrialization and beyond. COVID-19 has shot down the world economy with months. At the time of the AFTERMATH, the truth is many corporations and organizations will either have to upgrade to the INFORMATION AGE or disappear. More than the INFORMATION upgrade, the era of SOCIAL MEDIA and the MILLENNIALS are driving a revolution in the core philosophy of all organizations. Profit is not king anymore, support is. In this time and age where a teenager with a social account can compete with the million dollars PR firm, social implication is now the new cornerstone. Those who will adapt will prevail and prosper, while the resistance and old guards will soon be forgotten as fossils of a past era.

ALPHA LADDERS -075
CAPTAIN OF YOUR DESTINY
BY Dr. BAK NGUYEN & JONAS DIOP

In ALPHA LADDERS, Dr. Bak is sharing his private conversation and board meetings with 2 of his trusted lieutenants, strategist Jonas Diop and international Counsellor, Brenda Garcia. As both the Dr. Bak and ALPHA brands are gaining in popularity and traction, it was time to get the movement to the next level. Now, it's about building a community and to help everyone willing to become ALPHAS to find their powers. Dr. Bak is a natural recruiter of ALPHAS and peers. He also spent the last 20 years plus, training and mentoring proteges. Now comes the time to empower more and more proteges to become ALPHAS. ALPHAS LADDERS is the journey of how Dr. Bak went from a product of Conformity to rise into a force of Nature, know as a kind tornado. In ALPHA LADDERS Jonas pushed Dr. Bak to retrace each of the steps of his awakening, steps that we can breakdown and reproduce for ourselves. The goal is to empower each willing individual to become the ultimate Captain of his or her destiny, and to do it, again and again. Welcome to the Alphas.

ALPHA LADDERS 2 -081
SHAPING LEADERS AND ACHIEVERS
BY Dr. BAK NGUYEN & BRENDA GARCIA

In ALPHA LADDERS 2, Dr. Bak is sharing the second part of his private conversation and board meetings with his trusted lieutenants. This time it is with international Counsellor, Brenda Garcia that the dialogue is taking place. In this second tome, the journey is taken to the next level. If the first tome was about the WHYs and the HOWs at an individual level, this tome is about the WHYs and the HOWs at the societal level. Through the lens of her background in international relations and diplomacy, Brenda now has the mission to help Dr. Bak establish structures, not only for his emerging organization and legacy, THE ALPHAS, but to also inspire all the other leaders and structures of our society. To do this, Brenda is taking Dr. Bak on an anthropological, sociological and philosophical journey to revisit different historical key moments in various fields and eras, going as far back as in ancient Greece at the dawn of democracy, all the way to the golden era of modern multilateralism embodied by the UN structure. Learning from the legacies of prominent figures going from Plato to Ban Ki Moon, Martin Luther King or Nelson Mandela, to Machiavelli, Marx and Simone de Beauvoir, Brenda and Dr. Bak are attempting to grasp the essence of structure and hierarchy, their goal being to empower each willing individual to become the ultimate Captain of their own success, to climb up the ladders no matter how high it is, and to build their legacy one step at a time.

AMONGST THE ALPHAS -058
BY Dr. BAK NGUYEN, with Dr. MARIA KUNDSTATER, Dr. PAUL OUELLETTE and Dr. JEREMY KRELL

In AMONGST THE ALPHAS Dr. Bak opens the blueprint of the next level with the hope that everyone can be better, bigger, wiser, but above all, a philosophy of Life that if, well applied, can bring inspiration to life. The Alphas rose in the midst of the COVID war as an International Collaboration to empower individuals to rise from the global crisis. Joining Dr. Bak are some of the world thinkers and achievers, the Alphas. Doctors, business people, thinkers, achievers, influencers, they are coming together to define what is an Alpha and his or her role, making the world a better place. This isn't the American dream, it is the human dream, one that can help you make History.Joining Dr. Bak are 3 Alpha authors, Dr. Maria Kundstater, Dr. Paul Ouellette and Dr. Jeremy Krell. This book started with questions from coach Jonas Diop. Welcome to the Alphas.

AMONGST THE ALPHAS vol.2 -059
ON THE OTHER SIDE
BY Dr. BAK NGUYEN with Dr. JULIO REYNAFARJE, Dr. LINA DUSEVICIUTE and Dr. DUC-MINH LAM-DO

In AMONGST THE ALPHAS 2, Dr. Bak continues to explore the meaning of what it is to be an Alpha and how to act amongst Alphas, because as the saying taught us: alone one goes fast, together we goes far. Some people see the problem. Some people look at the problem, some people created the problem. Some people leverage the problem into solutions and opportunities. Well, all of those people are Alphas. Networking and leveraging one another, their powers and reach are beyond measure. And one will keep the other in line too. Joining Dr. Bak are 3 Alphas from around the world coming together to share and collaborate, Dr. DUSEVICIUTE, Dr. LAM-DO and Dr. REYNAFARJE. This isn't the American dream, it is the human dream, one that can help you make History. Welcome to the Alphas.

BOOTCAMP -071
BOOKS TO REWRITE MINDSETS INTO WINNING STATES OF MIND
BY Dr. BAK NGUYEN

In BOOTCAMP 8 BOOKS TO REWRITE MINDSETS INTO WINNING STATES OF MIND, Dr. Bak is taking you into his past, before the visionary entrepreneur, before the world records, before the Industry's disruptor status. Here are 8 of the books that changed Dr. Bak's thinking and, therefore, reset his evolution into the course we now know him for. BOOTCAMP: 8 BOOKS TO REWRITE MINDSETS INTO WINNING STATES OF MIND, is a Bootcamp of 8 weeks for anyone looking to experience Dr. Bak's training to become THE Dr. BAK you came to know and love. This book will summarize how each title changed Dr. Bak mindset into a state of mind and how he applied that to rewrite his destiny. 8 books to read, that's 8 weeks of Bootcamp to access the power of your MIND and of your WILL. Are you ready for a change?

BRANDING -044
BALANCING STRATEGY AND EMOTIONS
BY Dr. BAK NGUYEN

BRANDING is communication to its most powerful state. Branding is not just about communicating anymore but about making a promise, about establishing a relation, about generating an emotion. More than once, Dr. Bak proved himself to be a master, communicating and branding his ideas into flags attracting interest and influences, nationally and internationally. In BRANDING, Dr. Bak shares a very unique and personal journey, branding Dr. Bak. How does he go from Dr. Nguyen, a loved and respected dentist to becoming Dr. Bak, a world anchor hosting THE ALPHAS in the medical and financial world?More than a personal journey, BRANDING helps to break down the steps to elevate someone with nothing else but the force of his or her spirit. Welcome to the Alphas.

CHANGING THE WORLD FROM A DENTAL CHAIR -007
BY Dr. BAK NGUYEN

Since he has received the EY's nomination for entrepreneur of the year for his startup Mdex & Co, Dr. Bak Nguyen has pushed the opportunity to the next level. Speaker, author, and businessman, Dr. Bak is a true entrepreneur and industries' disruptor. To compensate for the startup's status of Mdex & Co, he challenged himself to write a book based on the EY's questionnaire to share an in-depth vision of his company. With "Changing the World from a dental chair" Dr. Bak is sharing his thought process and philosophy to his approach to the industry. Not looking to revolutionize but rather to empower, he became, despite himself, an industries disruptor: an entrepreneur who has established a new benchmark. Dr. Bak Nguyen is a cosmetic dentist and visionary businessman who won the GRAND HOMAGE prize of "LYS de la Diversité" 2016, for his contribution as a citizen and entrepreneur in the community. He also holds recognitions from the Canadian Parliament and the Canadian Senate.

In 2003, he founded Mdex, a dental company upon which in 2018, he launched the most ambitious private endeavour to reform the dental industry, Canada wide. He wrote seven books covering ENTREPRENEURSHIP, LEADERSHIP, QUEST of IDENTITY, and now, PROFESSION HEALTH. Philosopher, he has close to his heart the quest of happiness of the people surrounding him, patients, and colleagues alike. Those projects have allowed Dr. Nguyen to attract interests from the international and diplomatic community and he is now the centre of a global discussion on the wellbeing and the future of the health profession. It is in that matter that he shares with you his thoughts and encourages the health community to share their own stories.

CHAMPION MINDSET -039
LEARNING TO WIN
BY Dr. BAK NGUYEN & CHRISTOPHE MULUMBA

CHAMPION MINDSET is the encounter of the business world and the professional sports world. Industries' Disruptor Dr. BAK NGUYEN shares his wisdom and views with the HAMMER, CFL Football Star, Edmonton's Eskimos CHRISTOPHE MULUMBA on how to leverage on the champion mindset to create successful entrepreneurs. Writing and challenging each other, they discovered the parallels and the difference of both worlds, but mainly, the recipe for leveraging from one to succeed in the other, from champions and entrepreneurs to WINNERS. Build and score your millions, it is a matter of mindset! This is CHAMPION MINDSET.

EMPOWERMENT -069
BY Dr. BAK NGUYEN

In EMPOWERMENT, Dr. Bak's 69th book, writing a book every 8 days for 8 weeks in a row to write the next world record of writing 72 books/36 months, Dr. Bak is taking a rest, sharing his inner feelings, inspiration, and motivation. Much more than his dairy, EMPOWERMENT is the key to walk in his footsteps and to comprehend the process of an overachiever. Dr. Bak's helped and inspired countless people to find their voice, to live their dream, and to be the better version of themselves. Why is he sharing as much and keep sharing? Why is he going that fast, always further and further, why and how is he keeping his inspiration and momentum? Those are all the answers EMPOWERMENT will deliver to you. This book might be one of the fastest Dr. Bak has written, not because of time constraints but from inspiration, pure inspiration to share and to grow. There is always a dark side to each power, two faces to a coin. Well, this is the less prominent facets of Dr. Bak Momentum and success, the road to his MINDSET.

FORCES OF NATURE -015
FORGING THE CHARACTER OF WINNERS
BY Dr. BAK NGUYEN

In FORCES OF NATURE, Dr. Bak is giving his all. This is his 15 books written within 15 months. It is the end of a marathon to set the next world record. For the occasion, he wanted to end with a big bang! How about a book with all of his biggest challenges? A Quest of Identity, a journey looking for his name and powers, Dr. Bak is borrowing with myths and legends to make this journey universal. Yes, this is Dr. Bak's mythology. Demons, heroes and Gods, there are forces of Nature that we all meet on our way for our name. Some will scare us, some will fight us, some will manipulate us. We can flee, we can hide, we can fight. What we do will define our next encounter and the one after. A tale of personal growth, a journey to find power and purpose, Dr. Bak is showing us the path to freedom, the Path of Life. Welcome to the Alphas.

HORIZON, BUILDING UP THE VISION -045
VOLUME ONE
BY Dr. BAK NGUYEN

Dr. Bak is opening up at your demand! Many of you are following Dr. Bak online and are asking to know more about his lifestyle. This is how he has chosen to respond: sharing his lifestyle as he traveled the world and what he learned in each city to come to build his Mindset as a driver and a winner. Here are 10 destinations (over 69 that will be following in the next volumes...) in which he shares his journey. New York, Quebec, Paris, Punta Cana, Monaco, Los Angeles, Nice, Holguin, the journey happened over twenty years.

HORIZON, ON THE FOOTSTEP OF TITANS -048
VOLUME TWO
BY Dr. BAK NGUYEN

Dr. Bak is opening up at your demand! Many of you are following Dr. Bak online and are asking to know more about his lifestyle. This is how he has chosen to respond: sharing his lifestyle as he traveled the world and what he learned in each city to come to build his Mindset as a driver and a winner. Here are 9 destinations (over 72 that will be following in the next volumes...) in which he shares his journey. Hong Kong, London, Rome, San Francisco, Anaheim, and more..., the journey happened over twenty years. Dr. Bak is sharing with you his feelings, impressions, and how they shaped his state of mind and character into Dr. Bak. From a dreamer to a driver and a builder, the journey started since he was 3. Wealth is a state of mind, and a state of mind is the basis of the drive. Find out about the mind of an Industry's disruptor.

HORIZON, Dr.EAMING OF THE FUTURE -068
VOLUME THREE
BY Dr. BAK NGUYEN

Dr. Bak is back. From the midst of confinement, he remembers and writes about what life was, when traveling was a natural part of Life. It will come back. Now more than ever, we need to open both our hearts and minds to fight fear and intolerance. Writing from a time of crisis, he is sharing the magic and psychological effect of seeing the world and how it has shaped his mindset. Here are 9 other destinations (over 75) in which he shares his journey. Beijing, Key West, Madrid, Amsterdam, Marrakech and more..., the journey happened over twenty years.

HOW TO NOT FAIL AS A DENTIST -047
BY Dr. BAK NGUYEN

In HOW TO NOT FAIL AS A DENTIST, Dr. Bak is given 20 plus years of experience and knowledge of what it is to be a dentist on the ground. PROFESSIONAL INTELLIGENCE, FINANCIAL INTELLIGENCE and MANAGEMENT INTELLIGENCE are the fields that any dentist will have to master for a chance to success and a shot for happiness practicing dentistry. Where ever you are starting your career as a new graduate or a veteran in the field looking to reach the next level, this is book smart and street smart all into one. This is Million Dollar Mindset applied to dentistry. We won't be making a millionaire out of you from this book, we will be giving you a shot to happiness and success. The million will follow soon enough.

HOW TO WRITE A BOOK IN 30 DAYS -042
BY Dr. BAK NGUYEN

In HOW TO WRITE YOUR BOOK IN 30 DAYS, Dr. Bak has crafted writing skills and techniques that can be shared and mastered. This book is mainly about structure and how to keep moving forward, avoiding the hit of the INSPIRATION WALL. You will find a wealth of wisdom from his experience writing your first, second, or even 10th book. Dr. Bak is sharing his secrets writing books, having written himself 72 books within 36 months. Visionary businessman, doctor in dentistry, Dr. Bak describes himself as a Dentist by circumstances, a communicator by passion, and an entrepreneur by nature.

HOW TO WRITE A SUCCESSFUL BUSINESS PLAN -049
BY Dr. BAK NGUYEN & ROUBA SAKR

In HOW TO WRITE A SUCCESSFUL BUSINESS PLAN, Dr. Bak is given 20 plus years of experience and knowledge of what it is to be an entrepreneur and more importantly, how to have the investors and banks on your side. Being an entrepreneur is surely not something you learn from school, but there are steps to master so you can communicate your views and vision. That's the only way you will have financing. Writing a business is only not a mandatory stop only for the bankers, but an essential step to every entrepreneur, to know the direction and what's coming next. A business plan is also not set in stone, if there is a truth in business is that nothing will go as planned. Writing down your business plan the first time will prepare you to adapt and to overcome the challenges and surprises. For most entrepreneurs, a business is a passion. To most investors and all banks, a business is a system. Your business plan is the map to that system. However unique your ideas and business are, the mapping follows the same steps and pattern.

HUMILITY FOR SUCCESS -051
BALANCING STRATEGY AND EMOTIONS
BY Dr. BAK NGUYEN

HUMILITY FOR SUCCESS is exploring the emotional discomforts and challenges champions, and overachievers put themselves through. Success is never done overnight and on the way, just like the pain and the struggles aren't enough, we are dealing with the doubts, the haters, and those who like to tell us how to live our lives and what to do. At the same time, nothing of worth can be achieved alone. Every legend has a cast of characters, allies, mentors, companions, rivals, and foes. So one needs the key to social behaviour. HUMILITY FOR SUCCESS is exploring the matter and will help you sort out beliefs from values, peers from friends. Humility is much more about how we see ourselves than how others see us. For any entrepreneur and champion, our daily is to set our mindset right, and to perfect our skills, not to fit in. There is a world where CONFIDENCE grows is in synergy with HUMILITY. As you set the right label on the right belief, you will be able to grow and to leave the lies and haters far behinds. This is HUMILITY FOR SUCCESS.

HYBRID -011
THE MODERN QUEST OF IDENTITY
BY Dr. BAK NGUYEN

IDENTITY -004
THE ANTHOLOGY OF QUESTS
BY Dr. BAK NGUYEN

What if John Lennon was still alive and running for president today? What kind of campaign will he be running? IDENTIFY -THE ANTHOLOGY OF QUESTS is about the quest each of us has to undertake, sooner or later, THE QUEST OF IDENTITY. Citizen of the world, aim to be one, the one, one whole, one unity, made of many. That's the anthology of life! Start with your one, find your unity, and your legend will start. We are all small-minded people anyway! We need each other to be one! We need each other to be happy, so we, so you, so I, can be happy. This is the chorus of life. This is our song! Citizens of the world, I salute you! This is the first tome of the IDENTITY QUEST. FORCES OF NATURE (tome 2) will be following in SUMMER 2021. Also under development, Tome 3 - THE CONQUEROR WITHIN will start production soon.

INDUSTRIES DISRUPTORS -006
BY Dr. BAK NGUYEN

INDUSTRIES DISRUPTORS is a strange title, one that sparkles mixed feelings. A disruptor is someone making a difference, and since we, in general, do not like change, the label is mostly negative. But a disruptor is mostly someone who sees the same problem and challenge from another angle. The disruptor will tackle that angle and come up with something new from something existent. That's evolution! In INDUSTRIES DISRUPTORS, Dr. Bak is joining forces with James Stephan-Usypchuk to share with us what is going on in the minds and shoes of those entrepreneurs disrupting the old habits. Dr. Bak is changing the world from a dental chair, disrupting the dental, and now the book industry. James is a maverick in the Intelligence space, from marketing to Artificial Intelligence. Coming from very different backgrounds and industries, they end up telling very similar stories. If disruptors change the world, well, their story proves that disruptors can be made and forged. Here's the recipe. Here are their stories.

K

KRYPTO -040
TO SAVE THE WORLD
BY Dr. BAK NGUYEN & ILYAS BAKOUCH

L

LEADERSHIP -003
PANDORA'S BOX
BY Dr. BAK NGUYEN

LEADERSHIP, PANDORA'S BOX is 21 presidential speeches for a better tomorrow for all of us. It aims to drive HOPE and motivation into each and every one of us. Together we can make the difference, we hold such power. Covering themes from LOYALTY to GENEROSITY, from FREEDOM and INTELLIGENCE to DOUBTS and DEATH, this is not the typical presidential or motivational speeches that we are used to. LEADERSHIP PANDORA'S BOX will surf your emotions first, only to dive with you to touch the core and soul of our meaning: to matter. This is not a Quest of Identity, but the cry to rally as a species, to raise our heads toward the future, and to move forward as a WHOLE. Not a typical Dr. Bak's book, LEADERSHIP, PANDORA'S BOX is a must-read for all of you looking for hope and purpose, all of us, citizens of the world.

LEVERAGE -014
COMMUNICATION INTO SUCCESS

BY Dr. BAK NGUYEN

In LEVERAGE COMMUNICATION TO SUCCESS, Dr. Bak shares his secret and mindsets to elevate an idea into a vision and a vision into an endeavour. Some endeavours will be a project, some others will become companies, and some will grow into a movement. It does not matter, each started with great communication.Communication is a very vast concept, education, sale, sharing, empowering, coaching, preaching, entertaining. Those are all different kinds of communication. The intent differs, the audiences vary, the messages are unique but the frame can be templated and mastered. In LEVERAGE COMMUNICATION TO SUCCESS, Dr. Bak is loyal to his core, sharing only what he knows best, what he has done himself. This book is dedicated to communicating successfully in business.

M

MASTERMIND, 7 WAYS INTO THE BIG LEAGUE -052
BY Dr. BAK NGUYEN & JONAS DIOP

MASTERMIND, 7 WAYS INTO THE BIG LEAGUE is the result of the encounter of business coach Jonas Diop and Dr. Bak. As a professional podcaster and someone always seeking the truth and ways to leverage success and performance, coach Jonas is putting Dr. Bak to the test, one that should reveal his secret to overachieve month after month, accumulating a new world record every month. Follow those two great minds as they push each other to surpass themselves, each in their own way and own style. MASTERMIND, 7 WAYS INTO THE BIG LEAGUE is more than a roadmap to success, it is a journey and a live testimony as you are turning the pages, one by one.

MIDAS TOUCH -065
POST-COVID DENTISTRY
BY Dr. BAK NGUYEN, Dr. JULIO REYNAFARJE AND Dr. PAUL OUELLETTE

MIDAS TOUCH, is the memoir of what happened in the ALPHAS SUMMIT in the midst of the GREAT PAUSE as great minds throughout the world in the dental field are coming together. As the time of competition is obsolete, the new era of collaboration is blooming. This is the 3rd book of the ALPHAS, after AFTERMATH and RELEVANCY, all written in the midst of confinement. Dr. Julio Reynafarje is bearing this initiative, to share with you the secret of a successful and lasting relationship with your patients, balancing science and psychology, kindness, and professionalism. He personally invited the ALPHAS to join as co-author, Dr. Paul Ouellette, and Dr. Paul Dominique, and Dr. Bak.Together, they have more than 100 years of combined experience, wisdom, trade, skills, philosophy, and secrets to share with you to empower you in the rebuilding of the dental profession in the aftermath of COVID. RELEVANCY was about coming together and to rebuild the future. MIDAS TOUCH is about how to build, one treatment plan at a time, one story at a time, one smile at a time.

MINDSET ARMORY -050
BY Dr. BAK NGUYEN

MINDSET ARMORY is Dr. Bak's 49th book, days after he completed his world record of writing 48 books within 24 months, on top of being a CEO of Mdex & Co and a full-time cosmetic dentist. Dr. Bak is undoubtedly an OVERACHIEVER. From his last books, he has shared more and more of his lifestyle and how it forged his winning mindset. Within MINDSET ARMORY, Dr. Bak is sharing with us his tools, how he found them, forged them, and leverage them. Just like any warrior needs a shield, a sword, and a ride, here are Dr. Bak's. For any entrepreneur, the road to success is a long and winding journey. On the way, some will find allies and foes. Some allies will become foes, and some foes might become allies. In today's competitive world, the only constant is change. With the right tool, it is possible to achieve. The right tool, the right mindset. This is MINDSET ARMORY.

MIRROR -085
BY Dr. BAK NGUYEN

MIRROR is the theme for a personal book. Not only to Dr. Bak but to all of us looking to reach beyond who and what we actually are. MIRROR is special in the fact that it is not only the content of the book that is of worth but the process in which Dr. Bak shared his own evolution. To go beyond who we are, one must grow every day. And how do you compare your growth and how far have you reach? Looking in the mirror. In all of Dr. Bak's writing, looking at the past is a trap to avoid at all costs. Looking in the mirror, is that any better? Share Dr. Bak's way to push and keep pushing himself without friction nor resistance. Please read that again. To evolve without friction or resistance... that is the source of infinite growth and the unification of the Quest for Power and the Quest of Happiness.

MOMENTUM TRANSFER -009
BY Dr. BAK NGUYEN & Coach DINO MASSON

How to be successful in your business and in your life? Achieve Your Biggest Goals With MOMENTUM TRANSFER. START THE BUSINESS YOU WANT - AND BRING IT NEXT LEVEL! GET THE LIFE YOU ALWAYS WANTED - AND IMPROVE IT! TAKE ANY PROJECTS YOU HAVE - AND MAKE IT THE BEST! In this powerful book, you'll discover what a small business owner learned from a millionaire and successful entrepreneur. He applied his mentor's principles and is explaining them in full detail in this book. The small business owner wrote the book he has always wanted to read and went from the verge of bankruptcy to quadrupling his revenues in less than 9 months and improve his personal life by increasing his energy and bring back peacefulness. Together, the millionaire and the small business owner are sharing their most valuable business and life lessons to the world. The most powerful book to increase your momentum in your business and your life introduces simple and radical life-changing concepts: Multiply your business revenues by finding the Eye of your Momentum - Increase your energy by building and feeding your own Momentum - How to increase your confidence with these simple steps - How to transfer your new powerful energy into other aspects of your business and life - How to set goals and achieve them (even crush them!)- How to always tap into an effortless and limitless force within you- And much, much more!

PLAYBOOK INTRODUCTION -055
BY Dr. BAK NGUYEN

In PLAYBOOK INTRODUCTION, Dr. Bak is open the door to all the newcomers and aspirant entrepreneurs who are looking at where and when to start. Based on questions of two college students wanting to know how to start their entrepreneurial journey, Dr. Bak dives into his experiences to empower the next generation, not about what they should do, but how he, Dr. Bak, would have done it today. This is an important aspect to recognize in the business world, the world has changed since the INFORMATION AGE and the advent of the millenniums into the market. Most matrix and know-how have to be adapted to today's speed and accessibility to the information. We are living at the INFORMATION AGE, this book is the precursor to the ABUNDANCE AGE, at least to those open to embrace the opportunity.

PLAYBOOK INTRODUCTION 2 -056
BY Dr. BAK NGUYEN

In PLAYBOOK INTRODUCTION 2, Dr. Bak continuing the journey to welcome the newcomers and aspirant entrepreneurs looking at where and when to start. If the first volume covers the mindset, the second is covering much more in-depth the concept of debt and leverage. This is an important aspect to recognize in the business world, the world has changed since the INFORMATION AGE and the advent of the millenniums into the market. Most matrix and know-how have to be adapted to today's speed and accessibility to the information. We are living at the INFORMATION AGE, this book is the precursor to the ABUNDANCE AGE, at least to those open to embrace the opportunity.

POWER -043
EMOTIONAL INTELLIGENCE
BY Dr. BAK NGUYEN

IN POWER, EMOTIONAL INTELLIGENCE, Dr. Bak is sharing his experiences and secrets leveraging on his EMOTIONAL INTELLIGENCE, a power we all have within. From SYMPATHY, having others opening up to you, to ACTIVE LISTENING, saving you time and energy; from EMPATHY, allowing you to predict the future to INFLUENCE, enabling you to draft the future, not to forget the power of the crowd with MOMENTUM, you are now in possession of power in tune with nature, yourself. It is a unique take on the subject to empower you to find your powers and your destiny. Visionary businessman, doctor in dentistry, Dr. Bak describes himself as a Dentist by circumstances, a communicator by passion, and an entrepreneur by nature.

POWERPLAY -078
HOW TO BUILD THE PERFECT TEAM
BY Dr. BAK NGUYEN

In POWERPLAY, HOW TO BUILD THE PERFECT TEAM, Dr. Bak is sharing with you his experience, perspective, and mistake traveling the journey of the entrepreneur. A serial entrepreneur himself, he started venture only with a single partner as team to build companies with a director of human resources and a board of directors. POWERPLAY is not a story, it is the HOW TO build the perfect team, knowing that perfection is a lie. So how can one build a team that will empower his or her vision? How to recruit, how to train, how to retain? Those are all legitimate questions. And all of those won't matter if the first question isn't answered: what is the reason for the team? There is the old way to hire and the new way to recruit. Yes, Human Resources is all about mindset too! This journey is one of introspection, of leadership, and a cheat sheet to build, not only the perfect team but the team that will empower your legacy to the next level.

PROFESSION HEALTH - TOME ONE -005
THE UNCONVENTIONAL QUEST OF HAPPINESS
BY Dr. BAK NGUYEN, Dr. MIRJANA SINDOLIC, Dr. ROBERT DURAND AND COLLABORATORS

Why are health professionals burning out while they give the best of themselves to heal the world? Dr. Bak aims to break the curse of isolation that health professionals face and establish a conversation to start the healing process. PROFESSION HEALTH is the basis of an ongoing discussion and will also serve as an introduction to a study lead by Professor Robert Durand, DMD, MSc Science from University of Montreal, study co-financed by Mdex and the Federal Government of Canada. Co-writers are Dr. Mirjana Sindolic, Professor Robert Durand, Dr. Jean De Serres, MD and former President of Hema Quebec, Counsel-Minister Luis Maria Kalaff Sanchez, Dr. Miguel Angel Russo, MD, Banker Anthony Siggia, Banker Kyles Yves, and more...
This is the first Tome of three, dedicated to help "WHITE COATS" to heal and to find their happiness.

REBOOT -012
MIDLIFE CRISIS
BY Dr. BAK NGUYEN

MidLife Crisis is a common theme to each of us as we reach the threshold. As a man, as a woman, why is it that half of the marriages end up in recall? If anything else would have half those rates of failure, the lawsuits would be raining. Where are the flaws, the traps? Love is strong and pure, why is marriage not the reflection of that?

All hard to ask questions with little or no answers. Dr. Bak is sharing his reflections and findings as he reached himself the WALL OF MARRIAGE. This is a matter that affects all of our lives. It is time for some answers.

RELEVANCY - TOME TWO -064
REINVENTING OURSELVES TO SURVIVE
BY Dr. BAK NGUYEN & Dr. PAUL OUELLETTE AND COLLABORATORS

THE GREAT PAUSE was a reboot of all the systems of society. Many outdated systems will not make it back. The Dental Industry is a needed one, it has laid on complacency for far too long. In an age where expertise is global and democratized and can be replaced with technologies and artificial intelligence, the REBOOT will force, not just an update, but an operating system replacement and a firmware upgrade.First, they saved their industry with THE ALPHAS INITIATIVE, sharing their knowledge and vision freely to all the world's dental industry. With the OUELLETTE INITIATIVE, they bought some time to all the dental clinics to resume and to adjust. The warning has been given, the clock is now ticking. who will prevail and prosper and who will be left behind, outdated and obsolete?

RISING -062
TO WIN MORE THAN YOU ARE AFRAID TO LOSE
BY Dr. BAK NGUYEN

In RISING, TO WIN MORE TAN YOU ARE AFRAID TO LOSE, Dr. Bak is breaking down the strategy to success to all, not only those wearing white coats and scrubs. More than his previous book (SUCCESS IS A CHOICE), this one is covering most of the aspects of getting to the next level, psychologically, socially, and financially. Rising is broken down into three key strategies: Financial Leverage - Compressing time - Always being in control. Presented by MILLION DOLLAR MINDSET, the book is covering more than the ways to create wealth, but also how to reach happiness and to live a life without regrets. Dr. Bak the CEO and founder of Mdex & Co, a company with the promise of reforming the whole dental industry for the better. He wrote more than 60 books within 30 months as he is sharing his experiences, secrets, and wisdom.

S

SELFMADE -036
GRATITUDE AND HUMILITY
BY Dr. BAK NGUYEN

This is the story of Dr. Bak, an artist who became a dentist, a dentist who became an Entrepreneur, an Entrepreneur who is seeking to save an entire industry. In his free time, Dr. Bak managed to write 37 books and is a contender to 3 world records to be confirmed. Businessman and visionary, his views and philosophy are ahead of our time. This is his 37th book. In SELFMADE, Dr. Bak is answering the questions most entrepreneurs want to know, the HOWTO and the secret recipes, not just to succeed, but to keep going no matter what! SELFMADE is the perfect read for any entrepreneurs, novices, and veterans.

SUCCESS IS A CHOICE -060
BLUEPRINTS FOR HEALTH PROFESSIONALS
BY Dr. BAK NGUYEN

In SUCCESS IS A CHOICE, FINANCIAL MILLIONAIRE BLUEPRINTS FOR HEALTH PROFESSIONALS, Dr. Bak is breaking down the strategy to success for all those wearing white coats and scrubs: doctors, dentists, pharmacists, chiropractors, nurses, etc. Success is broken down into three key strategies: Financial Leverage - Compressing time - Always being in control. Presented by MILLION DOLLAR MINDSET, the book is covering more than the ways to create wealth, but also how to reach happiness and to live a life without regrets. Dr. Bak is a successful cosmetic dentist with nearly 20 years of experience. He founded Mdex & Co, a company with the promise of reforming the whole dental industry for the better. While doing so, he discovered a passion for writing and for sharing. Multiple times World Record, Dr. Bak is writing a book every 2 weeks for the last 30 months. This is his 60th book, and he is still practicing. How he does it, is what he is sharing with us, SUCCESS, HAPPINESS, and mostly FREEDOM to all Health Professionals.

SYMPHONY OF SKILLS -001
BY Dr. BAK NGUYEN

You will enlighten the world with your potential. I can't wait to see all the differences that you will have in our world. Remember that power comes with responsibility. We can feel in his presence, a genuine force, a depth of energy, confidence, innocence, courage, and intelligence. Bak is always looking for answers, morning and night, he wants to understand the why and the why not. This book is the essence of the man. Dr. Bak is a force of nature who bears proudly his title eHappy. The man never ceases smiling nor spreading his good vibe wherever he passes. He is not trapped in the nostalgia of the past nor the satisfaction of the present, he embodies the joy of what's possible, what's to come. The more we read, the more we share, and we live. That is Bak, he charms us to evolve and to share his points of view, and before we know it, we are walking by his side, a journey we never saw coming.

T

THE 90 DAYS CHALLENGE -061
BY Dr. BAK NGUYEN

THE 90 DAYS CHALLENGE, is Dr. Bak's journey into the unknown. Overachiever writing 2 books a month on average, for the last 30 months, ambitious CEO, Industries' Disruptor, Dr. Bak seems to have success in everything he touches. Everything except the control of his weight. For nearly 20 years, he struggles with an overweight problem. Every time he scored big, he added on a little more weight. Well, this time, he exposes himself out there, in real-time and without filter, accepting the challenge of his brother-in-law, DON VO to lose 45 pounds within 90 days. That's half a pound a day, for three months. He will have to do so while keeping all of his other challenges on track, writing books at a world record pace, leading the dental industry into the new ERA, and keep seeing his patients. Undoubtedly entertaining, this is the journey of an ALPHA who simply won't give up. But this time, nothing is sure.

THE BOOK OF LEGENDS -024
BY Dr. BAK NGUYEN & WILLIAM BAK

The Book of Legends vol. 1 the story behind the world record of Dr. Bak and his son, William Bak. All Dr. Bak had in mind was to keep his promise of writing a book with his son. They ended up writing 8 children's books within a month, scoring a new world record. William is also the youngest author having published in two languages. Those are world records waiting to be confirmed. History will say: to celebrate a first world record (writing 15 books / 15 months), for the love of his son, he will have scored a second world record: to write 8 books within a month! THE BOOK OF LEGENDS vol. 1 This is both a magical journey for both a father and a son looking to connect and to find themselves. Join Dr. Bak and William Bak in their journey and their love for Life!

THE BOOK OF LEGENDS 2 -041
BY Dr. BAK NGUYEN & WILLIAM BAK

THE BOOK OF LEGENDS vol. 2 is the sequel of "CINDERELLA" but a true story between a father and his son. Together they have discovered a bond and a way to connect. The first BOOK OF LEGENDS covered the time of the first four books they wrote together within a month. The second BOOK OF LEGENDS is covering what happened after the curtains dropped, what happened after reality kicked back in. If the first volume was about a fairy tale in vacation time, the second volume is about making it last in real Life. Share their journey and their love of Life!

THE BOOK OF LEGENDS 3 -086
THE END OF THE INNOCENCE AGE
BY Dr. BAK NGUYEN & WILLIAM BAK

This is the third volume of the series, THE BOOK OF LEGENDS. If the first two happened as a breeze breaking world records on top of world records (27 books written as father and son), the 3rd volume took much more time to arrive. William has grown and writing chicken books is not enough anymore to ignite his imagination. Dr. Bak, as a good father, will try to follow William's growth and invented new games, technics and mind frames to keep engaging William's imagination and interest. From auditions to backstories, Dr. Bak bent backward to keep the adventure going. More than sharing the success and the glory, within THE BOOK OF LEGENDS volume 3, you are sharing the doubts and failure of a father and son refusing to let go... but who have now left MOMENTUM... until the winds blow once more in their favour. Welcome to the Alphas.

THE CONFESSION OF A LAZY OVERACHIEVER -089
REINVENT YOURSELF FROM ANY CRISIS
BY Dr. BAK NGUYEN

In THE CONFESSION OF A LAZY OVERACHIEVER, Dr. Bak is opening up to his new marketing officer, Jamie, fresh out of school. She is young, full of energy, and looking to chill and still to have it all. True to his character, Dr. Bak is giving Jamie some leeway to redefine Dr. Bak's brand to her demographic, the Millennials. This journey is about Dr. Bak satisfying the Millennials and answering their true questions in life. A rebel himself, his ambition to change the world started back on campus, some 25 years ago... then, life caught up with him. It took Dr. Bak 20 years to shake down the burdens of life, to spread his wings free from Conformity, and to start Overachieving. Doctor, CEO, and world record author, here is what Dr. Bak would have love to know 25 years ago as was still on campus. In a word, this is cheating your way to success and freedom. And yes, it is possible. Success, Money, Freedom, it all starts with a mindset and the awareness of Time. Welcome to the Alphas.

THE ENERGY FORMULA -053
BY Dr. BAK NGUYEN

THE ENERGY FORMULA is a book dedicated to help each individual to find the means to reach their purpose and goal in Life. Dr. Bak is a philosopher, a strategist, a business, an artist, and a dentist, how does he do all of that? He is doing so while mentoring proteges and leading the modernization of an entire industry. Until now, Momentum and Speed were the powers that he was building on and from. But those powers come from somewhere too. From a guide of our Quest of Identity, he became an ally in everyone's journey for happiness. THE ENERGY FORMULA is the book revealing step by step, the logic of building the right mindset and the way to ABUNDANCE and HAPPINESS, universally. It is not just a HOW TO book, but one that will change your life and guide you to the path of ABUNDANCE.

THE MODERN WOMAN -070
TO HAVE IT HAVE WITH NO SACRIFICE
BY Dr. BAK NGUYEN & Dr. EMILY LETRAN

In THE MODERN WOMAN: TO HAVE IT ALL WITH NO SACRIFICE, Dr. Bak joins forces with Dr. Emily Letran to empower all women to fulfill their desires, goals, and ambition. Both overachievers going against the odds, they are sharing their experience and wisdom to help all women to find confidence and support to redefine their lives. Dr. Emily Letran is a doctor in dentistry, an entrepreneur, author, and CERTIFIED HIGH-PERFORMANCE coach. For an Asian woman, she made it through the norms and the red tapes to find her voice. As she learned and grew with mentors, today she is sharing her secret with the energy that will motivate all of the female genders to stand for what they deserve. Alpha doctor, Bak is joining his voice and perspective since this is not about gender equality, but about personal empowerment and the quest of Identity of each, man and woman. Once more, Dr. Bak is bringing LEVERAGE and REASON to the new social deal between man and woman. This is not about gender, but about confidence.

THE POWER BEHIND THE ALPHA -008
BY TRANIE VO & Dr. BAK NGUYEN

It's been said by a "great man" that "We are born alone and we die alone." Both men and women proudly repeat those words as wisdom since. I apologize in advance, but what a fat LIE! That's what I learned and discovered in life since my mind and heart got liberated from the burden of scars and the ladders of society. I can have it all, not all at the same time, but I can have everything I put my mind and heart into. Actually, it is not completely true. I can have most of what I and Tranie put our minds into. Together, when we feel like one, there isn't much out of our reach. If I'm the mind, she's the heart; if I'm the Will, she's the means. Synergy is the core of our power.Tranie's aim is always Happiness. In Tranie's definition of life, there are no justifications, no excuses, no tomorrow. For Tranie, Happiness is measured by the minutes of every single day. This is why she's so strong and can heal people around her. That may also be why she doesn't need to talk much, since talking about the past or the future is, in her mind, dimming down the magic of the present, the Now. We both respect and appreciate that we are the whole balancing each other's equation of life, of love, of success. I was the plus and the minus, then I became the multiplication factor and grew into the exponential. And how is Tranie evolving in all of this? She is and always will be the balance. If anything, she is the equal sign of each equation.

THE POWER OF Dr. -066
THE MODERN TITLE OF NOBILITY
BY Dr. BAK NGUYEN, Dr. PAVEL KRASTEV AND COLLABORATORS

In THE POWER OF Dr., independent thinkers mean to exchange ideas. An idea can be very powerful if supported with a great work ethic. Work ethic, isn't that the main fabric of our white coats, scrubs, and title? In an era post-COVID where everything has been rebooted and that the healthcare industry is facing its own fate: to evolve or to be replaced, Dr. Bak and Dr. Pavel reveal the source of their power and their playbook to move forward, ahead.The power we all hold is our resilience and discipline. We put that for years at the service of our profession, from a surgical perspective. Now, we can harness that same power to rewrite the rules, the industry, and our future. Post-COVID, the rules are being rewritten, will you be part of the team or left behind?
"You can be in control!" More than personal growth and a motivational book, THE POWER OF Dr. is an awakening call to the doctor you look at when you graduate, with hope, with honour, with determination.

THE POWER OF YES -010
VOLUME ONE: IMPACT
BY Dr. BAK NGUYEN

In THE POWER OF YES, Dr. Bak is sharing his journey opening up and embracing the world, one day at a time, one ask at a time, one wish at a time. Far from a dare, saying YES allowed Dr. Bak to rewrite his mindsets and to break all the boundaries. This book is not one written a few days or weeks, but the accumulation of a journey for 12 months. The journeys started as Dr. Bak said YES to his producer to go on stage and to speak... That YES opened a world of possibilities. Dr. Bak embraced each and every one of them. 12 months later, he is celebrating the new world record of writing 9 books written over a period of 12 months. To him, it will be a miss, missing the 12 on 12 mark. To the rest of the world, they just saw the birth of a force of nature, the Alpha force. THE POWER OF YES is comprised of all the introduction of the adult books written by Dr. Bak within the first 12 months. Chapter by chapter, you can walk in his footstep seeing and smelling what he has. This is reality literature with a twist of POWER. THE POWER OF YES! Discover your potential and your power. This is the POWER OF YES, volume one. Welcome to the Alphas.

THE POWER OF YES 2 -037
VOLUME TWO: SHAPELESS
BY Dr. BAK NGUYEN

In THE POWER OF YES, volume 2, Dr. Bak is continuing his journey discovering his powers and influence. After 12 months embracing the world saying YES, he rose as an emerging force: he's been recognized as an INDUSTRIES DISRUPTOR, got nominated ERNST AND YOUNG ENTREPRENEUR OF THE YEAR, wrote 9 books within 12 months while launching the most ambitious private endeavour to reform his own industry, the dental field. Contender too many WORLD RECORDS, Dr. Bak is doing all of that in parallel. And yes, he is sleeping his nights and yes, he is writing his book himself, from the screen of his iPhone! Far from satisfied, Dr. Bak missed the mark of writing 12 books within 12 months and everything else is shaping and moving, and could come crumbling down at each turn. Now that Dr. Bak understands his powers, he is looking to test them and to push them to their limits, looking to keep scoring world records while materializing his vision and enterprises. This is the awakening of a Force of Nature looking to change the world for the better while having fun sharing. Welcome to the Alphas.

THE POWER OF YES 3 -046
VOLUME THREE: LIMITLESS
BY Dr. BAK NGUYEN

In THE POWER OF YES, volume 3, the journey of Dr. Bak continues where the last volume left, in front of 300 plus people showing up to his first solo event, a Dr. Bak's event. On stage and in this book, Dr. Bak reveals how 12 months saying YES to everything changed his life... actually, it was 18 months.
From a dentist looking to change the world from a dental chair into a multiple times world record author, the journey of openness is a rendez-vous with Fate. Dr. Bak is sharing almost in real-time his journey, experiences, but above all, his feelings, doubts, and comebacks. From one book to the next, from one journey to the next, follow the adventure of a man looking to find his name, his worth, and his place in the world. Doing so, he is touching people Doing so, he is touching people and initiating their rises. Are you ready for more? Are you ready to meet your Fate and Destiny? Welcome to the Alphas.

THE POWER OF YES 4 -087
VOLUME FOUR: PURPOSE
BY Dr. BAK NGUYEN

In THE POWER OF YES, volume 4, the journey continues days after where the last volume left. After setting the new world record of writing 48 books within 24 months, Dr. Bak is not ready to stop. As volume one covers 12 months of journey, volume 2 covers 6 months. Well, volume 3 covers 4 months. The speed is building up and increasing, steadily. This is volume 4, RISING, after breaking the sound barrier. Dr. Bak has reached a state where he is above most resistance and friction, he is now in a universe of his own, discovering his powers as he walks his journeys. This is no fiction story or wishful thinking, THE POWER OF YES is the journey of Dr. Bak, from one world record to the next, from one book to the next. You too can walk your own legend, you just need to listen to your innersole and to open up to the opportunity. May you get inspiration from the legendary journey of Dr. Bak and find your own Destiny. Welcome to the Alphas.

THE RISE OF THE UNICORN -038
BY Dr. BAK NGUYEN & Dr. JEAN DE SERRES

In THE RISE OF THE UNICORN, Dr. Bak is joining forces with his friend and mentor, Dr. Jean De Serres. Together both men had many achievements in their respective industries, but the advent of eHappyPedia, THE RISE OF THE UNICORN is a personal project dear to both of them: the QUEST OF HAPPINESS and its empowerment. This book is a special one since you are witnessing the conversation between two entrepreneurs looking to change the world by building unique tools and media. Just like any enterprise, the ride is never a smooth one in the park on a beautiful day. But this is about eHappyPedia, it is about happiness, right? So it will happen and with a smile attached to it! The unique value of this book is that you are sharing the ups and downs of the launch of a Unicorn, not just the glory of the fame, but also the doubts and challenges on the way. May it inspire you on your own journey to success and happiness.

THE RISE OF THE UNICORN 2 -076
eHappyPedia
BY Dr. BAK NGUYEN & Dr. JEAN DE SERRES

This is 2 years after starting the first tome. Dr. Bak's brand is picking up, between the accumulation of records and the recognition. eHappyPedia is now hot for a comeback. In THE RISE OF THE UNICORN 2, Dr. Bak is retracing and addressing each of Dr. Jean De Serres' concerns about the weakness of the first version of eHappyPedia and the eHappy movement. This is the sort of the creation and a UNICORN both in finance and in psychology. Never before, you will assist in such daily and decision-making process of a world phenomenon and of a company. Dr. Bak and Dr. De Serres are literally using the process of writing this series of books to plan and to brainstorm the birth of a bluechip. More than an intriguing story, this is the journey of 2 experienced entrepreneurs changing the world.

THE U.A.X STORY -072
THE ULTIMATE AUDIO EXPERIENCE
BY Dr. BAK NGUYEN

This is the story of the ULTIMATE AUDIO EXPERIENCE, U.A.X. Follow Dr. Bak's footstep on how he invented a new way to read and to learn. Dr. Bak brings his experience as a movie producer and a director to elevate the reading experience to another level with entertaining value and make it accessible to everyone, auditive, and visual people alike.

Three years plus of research and development, countless hours of trials and errors, Dr. Bak finally solved his puzzle: having written more than 1.1 million words. The irony is that he does not like to read, he likes audiobooks! U.A.X. finally allowed the opening of Dr. Bak's entire library to a new genre and media. U.A.X. is the new way to learn and enjoy Audiobooks. Made to be entertaining while keeping the self-educational value of a book, U.A.X. will appeal to both auditive and visual people. U.A.X. is the blockbuster of the Audiobooks. The format has already been approved by iTunes, Amazon, Spotify, and all major platforms for global distribution and streaming.

THE VACCINE -077
BY Dr. BAK NGUYEN & WILLIAM BAK

In THE VACCINE, A TALE OF SPIES AND ALIENS, Dr. Bak reprise his role as mentor to William, his 10 years-old son, both as co-author and as doctor. William is living through the COVID war and has accumulated many, many questions. That morning, they got out all at once. From a conversation between father and son, Dr. Bak is making science into words keeping the interest of his son a Saturday morning in bed. William is not just an audience, he is responsible to map the field with his questions. What started as a morning conversation between father and son, became within the next hour, a great project, their 23rd book together. Learn about the virus, vaccination while entertaining your kids.

TO OVERACHIEVE EVERYTHING BEING LAZY -090
CHEAT YOUR WAY TO SUCCESS
BY Dr. BAK NGUYEN

In TO OVERACHIEVE EVERYTHING BEING LAZY, Dr. Bak retaking his role talking to the millennials, the next generation. If in the first tome of the series LAZY, Dr. Bak addresses the general audience of millennials, especially young women, he is dedicating this tome to the ALPHA amongst the millennials, those aiming for the moon and looking, not only to be happy but to change the world. This is not another take on how to cheat your way to success or how to leverage laziness, but this is the recipe to build overachievers and rainmakers. For the young leaders with ambitions and talent, understanding TIME and ENERGY are crucial from your first steps writing your our legend. If Dr. Bak had the chance to do it all over again, this is how he would do it! Welcome to the Alphas.

TORNADO -067
FORCE OF CHANGE
BY Dr. BAK NGUYEN

In TORNADO - FORCE OF CHANGE Dr. Bak is writing solo. In the midst of the COVID war, change is not a good intention anymore. Change, constant change has become a new reality, a new norm. From somebody who holds the title of Industries' Disruptor, how does he yield change to stay in control? Well, the changes from the COVID war are constant fear and much loss of individual liberty. Some can endure the change, some will ride it. Dr. Bak is sharing his angle of navigating the changes, yielding the improvisations, and to reinvent the goals, the means to stay relevant. From fighting to keep his companies Dr. Bak went on to let go the uncontrollable to embrace the opportunity, he reinvented himself to ride the change and create opportunities from an unprecedented crisis. This is the story of a man refusing to kneel and accept defeat, smiling back at faith to find leverage and hope.

TOUCHSTONE -073
LEVERAGING TODAY'S PSYCHOLOGICAL SMOG
BY Dr. BAK NGUYEN & Dr. KEN SEROTA

TOUCHSTONE, LEVERAGING TODAY'S PSYCHOLOGICAL SMOG is mapping to navigate and to thrive in today's high and constant stress environment. After 40 years in practice, Dr. Serota is concerned about the evolution of the career of health care professionals and the never-ending level of stress. What is stress, what are its effects, damages, and symptoms? If COVID-19 revealed to the world that we are fragile, it also revealed most of the broken and the flaws of our system. For now a century, dentistry has been a champion in depression, Dr.ug addiction, and suicide rate, and the curve is far from flattening. Dr. Bak is sharing his perspective and experience dealing with stress and how to leverage it into a constructive force. From the stress of a doctor with no right to failure to the stress of an entrepreneur never knowing the future, Dr. Bak is sharing his way to use stress as leverage.

ABOUT THE AUTHORS

From Canada, **Dr BAK NGUYEN,** Nominee Ernst and Young Entrepreneur of the year, Grand Homage Lys DIVERSITY, and LinkedIn & TownHall Achiever of the year. Dr Bak is a cosmetic dentist, CEO and founder of Mdex & Co. His company is revolutionizing the dental field. Speaker and motivator, he wrote 72 books over 36 months accumulating many world records (to be officialized).

- **ENTREPRENEURSHIP**
- **LEADERSHIP**
- **QUEST OF IDENTITY**
- **DENTISTRY AND MEDICINE**
- **PARENTING**
- **CHILDREN BOOKS**
- **PHILOSOPHY**

In 2003, he founded Mdex, a dental company upon which in 2018, he launched the most ambitious private endeavour to reform the dental industry, Canada wide. Philosopher, he has close to his heart the quest of happiness of the people surrounding him, patients and colleagues alike. In 2020, he launched an International collaborative initiative named **THE ALPHAS** to share knowledge and for Entrepreneurs and Doctors to thrive through the Greatest Pandemic and Economic depression of our time.

In 2016, he co-found with Tranie Vo, Emotive World Incorporated, a tech research company to use technology to empower happiness and sharing. U.A.X. the ultimate audio experience is the landmark project on which the team is advancing, utilizing the technics of the movie industry and the advancement in ARTIFICIAL INTELLIGENCE to save the book industry and to upgrade the continuing education space.

These projects have allowed Dr Nguyen to attract interests from the international and diplomatic community and he is now the center of a global discussion in the wellbeing and the future of the health profession. It is in that matter that he shares his thoughts and encourages the health community to share their own stories.

> "It's not worth it go through it alone! Together, we stand, alone, we fall."

Motivational speaker and serial entrepreneur, philosopher and author, from his own words, Dr Nguyen describes himself as a dentist by circumstances, an entrepreneur by nature and a communicator by passion.

He also holds recognitions from the Canadian Parliament and the Canadian Senate.

www.DrBakNguyen.com

AMAZON - BARNES & NOBLE - APPLE BOOKS - KINDLE
SPOTIFY - APPLE MUSIC

ULTIMATE AUDIO EXPERIENCE

A new way to learn and enjoy Audiobooks. Made to be entertaining while keeping the self-educational value of a book, UAX will appeal to both auditive and visual people. UAX is the blockbuster of the Audiobooks.

UAX will cover most of Dr Bak's books, and is now negotiating to bring more authors and more titles to the UAX concept. Now streaming on Spotify, Apple Music and available for download on all major music platforms. Give it a try today!

AMAZON - BARNES & NOBLE - APPLE BOOKS - KINDLE
SPOTIFY - APPLE MUSIC

FROM THE SAME AUTHOR
Dr. Bak Nguyen

TITLES AVAILABLE AT
www.DrBakNguyen.com

MAJOR LEAGUES' ACCESS

FACTEUR HUMAIN -035
LE LEADERSHIP DU SUCCÈS
par Dr. BAK NGUYEN & CHRISTIAN TRUDEAU

THE RISE OF THE UNICORN -038
BY Dr. BAK NGUYEN & Dr. JEAN DE SERRES

CHAMPION MINDSET -039
LEARNING TO WIN
BY Dr. BAK NGUYEN & CHRISTOPHE MULUMBA

THE RISE OF THE UNICORN 2 -076
eHappyPedia
BY Dr. BAK NGUYEN & Dr. JEAN DE SERRES

BRANDING -044
BALANCING STRATEGY AND EMOTIONS
BY Dr. BAK NGUYEN

002 - **La Symphonie des Sens**
ENTREPREUNARIAT
par Dr. BAK NGUYEN

006 - **INDUSTRIES DISRUPTORS**
BY Dr. BAK NGUYEN

007 - **Changing the World from a dental chair**
BY Dr. BAK NGUYEN

008 - **The Power Behind the Alpha**
BY TRANIE VO & Dr. BAK NGUYEN

036 - **SELFMADE**
GRATITUDE AND HUMILITY
BY Dr. BAK NGUYEN

072 - **THE U.A.X. STORY**
THE ULTIMATE AUDIO EXPERIENCE
BY Dr. BAK NGUYEN

088 - **CRYPTOCONOMICS 101**
MY PERSONAL JOURNEY
FROM 50K TO 1 MILLION
BY Dr BAK NGUYEN

BUSINESS

SYMPHONY OF SKILLS -001
BY Dr. BAK NGUYEN

CHILDREN'S BOOK
with William Bak

The Trilogy of Legends

THE LEGEND OF THE CHICKEN HEART -016
LA LÉGENDE DU COEUR DE POULET -017
BY Dr. BAK NGUYEN & WILLIAM BAK

THE LEGEND OF THE LION HEART -018
LA LÉGENDE DU COEUR DE LION -019
BY Dr. BAK NGUYEN & WILLIAM BAK

THE LEGEND OF THE DRAGON HEART -020
LA LÉGENDE DU COEUR DE DRAGON -021
BY Dr. BAK NGUYEN & WILLIAM BAK

WE ARE ALL DRAGONS -022
NOUS TOUS, DRAGONS -023
BY Dr. BAK NGUYEN & WILLIAM BAK

The Collection of the Chicken

THE 9 SECRETS OF THE SMART CHICKEN -025
LES 9 SECRETS DU POULET INTELLIGENT -026
BY Dr. BAK NGUYEN & WILLIAM BAK

THE SECRET OF THE FAST CHICKEN -027
LE SECRETS DU POULET RAPIDE -028
BY Dr. BAK NGUYEN & WILLIAM BAK

THE LEGEND OF THE SUPER CHICKEN -029
LA LÉGENDE DU SUPER POULET -030
BY Dr. BAK NGUYEN & WILLIAM BAK

031- **THE STORY OF THE CHICKEN SHIT**
032- **L'HISTOIRE DU CACA DE POULET**
BY Dr. BAK NGUYEN & WILLIAM BAK

033- **WHY CHICKEN CAN'T DREAM?**
034- **POURQUOI LES POULETS NE RÊVENT PAS?**
BY Dr. BAK NGUYEN & WILLIAM BAK

057- **THE STORY OF THE CHICKEN NUGGET**
083- **HISTOIRE DE POULET: LA PÉPITE**
BY Dr. BAK NGUYEN & WILLIAM BAK

082- **CHICKEN FOREVER**
084- **POULET POUR TOUJOURS**
BY Dr BAK NGUYEN & WILLIAM BAK

THE SPIES AND ALIENS COLLECTION

077- **THE VACCINE**
079- **LE VACCIN**
077B- **LA VACUNA**
BY Dr BAK NGUYEN & WILLIAM BAK
TRANSLATION BY BRENDA GARCIA

DENTISTRY

PROFESSION HEALTH - TOME ONE -005
THE UNCONVENTIONAL
QUEST OF HAPPINESS
BY Dr. BAK NGUYEN, Dr. MIRJANA SINDOLIC,
Dr. ROBERT DURAND AND COLLABORATORS

HOW TO NOT FAIL AS A DENTIST -047
BY Dr. BAK NGUYEN

SUCCESS IS A CHOICE -060
BLUEPRINTS FOR HEALTH
PROFESSIONALS
BY Dr. BAK NGUYEN

RELEVANCY - TOME TWO -064
REINVENTING OURSELVES TO SURVIVE
BY Dr. BAK NGUYEN & Dr. PAUL OUELLETTE AND
COLLABORATORS

MIDAS TOUCH -065
POST-COVID DENTISTRY
BY Dr. BAK NGUYEN, Dr. JULIO REYNAFARJE AND
Dr. PAUL OUELLETTE

THE POWER OF DR -066
THE MODERN TITLE OF NOBILITY
BY Dr. BAK NGUYEN, Dr. PAVEL KRASTEV AND
COLLABORATORS

QUEST OF IDENTITY

004- **IDENTITY**
THE ANTHOLOGY OF QUESTS
BY Dr. BAK NGUYEN

011- **HYBRID**
THE MODERN QUEST OF IDENTITY
BY Dr. BAK NGUYEN

LIFESTYLE

045- **HORIZON, BUILDING UP THE VISION**
VOLUME ONE
BY Dr. BAK NGUYEN

048- **HORIZON, ON THE FOOTSTEPS OF TITANS**
VOLUME TWO
BY Dr. BAK NGUYEN

068- **HORIZON, DREAMING OF TRAVELING**
VOLUME THREE
BY Dr. BAK NGUYEN

MILLION DOLLAR MINDSET

MOMENTUM TRANSFER -009
BY Dr. BAK NGUYEN & Coach DINO MASSON

LEVERAGE -014
COMMUNICATION INTO SUCCESS
BY Dr. BAK NGUYEN AND COLLABORATORS

HOW TO WRITE A BOOK IN 30 DAYS -042
BY Dr. BAK NGUYEN

POWER -043
EMOTIONAL INTELLIGENCE
BY Dr. BAK NGUYEN

HOW TO WRITE A SUCCESSFUL BUSINESS PLAN -049
BY Dr BAK NGUYEN & ROUBA SAKR

MINDSET ARMORY -050
BY Dr. BAK NGUYEN

MASTERMIND, 7 WAYS INTO THE BIG LEAGUE -052
BY Dr. BAK NGUYEN & JONAS DIOP

PLAYBOOK INTRODUCTION -055
BY Dr. BAK NGUYEN

PLAYBOOK INTRODUCTION 2 -056
BY Dr. BAK NGUYEN

062- **RISING**
TO WIN MORE THAN YOU ARE AFRAID TO LOSE
BY Dr. BAK NGUYEN

067- **TORNADO**
FORCE OF CHANGE
BY Dr. BAK NGUYEN

071- **BOOTCAMP**
BOOKS TO REWRITE MINDSETS INTO WINNING STATES OF MIND
BY Dr. BAK NGUYEN

078- **POWERPLAY**
HOW TO BUILD THE PERFECT TEAM
BY Dr. BAK NGUYEN

PARENTING

024- **THE BOOK OF LEGENDS**
BY Dr. BAK NGUYEN & WILLIAM BAK

041- **THE BOOK OF LEGENDS 2**
BY Dr. BAK NGUYEN & WILLIAM BAK

086- **THE BOOK OF LEGENDS 3**
THE END OF THE INNOCENCE AGE
BY Dr. BAK NGUYEN & WILLIAM BAK

PERSONAL GROWTH

REBOOT -012
MIDLIFE CRISIS
BY Dr. BAK NGUYEN

HUMILITY FOR SUCCESS -051
BALANCING STRATEGY AND EMOTIONS
BY Dr. BAK NGUYEN

THE ENERGY FORMULA -053
BY Dr. BAK NGUYEN

AMONGST THE ALPHA -058
BY Dr. BAK NGUYEN & COACH JONAS DIOP

AMONGST THE ALPHA vol.2 -059
ON THE OTHER SIDE
BY Dr. BAK NGUYEN & COACH JONAS DIOP

THE 90 DAYS CHALLENGE -061
BY Dr. BAK NGUYEN

EMPOWERMENT -069
BY Dr BAK NGUYEN

THE MODERN WOMAN -070
TO HAVE IT HAVE WITH NO SACRIFICE
BY Dr. BAK NGUYEN & Dr. EMILY LETRAN

ALPHA LADDERS -075
CAPTAIN OF YOUR DESTINY
BY Dr BAK NGUYEN & JONAS DIOP

080- **1SELF**
REINVENT YOURSELF
FROM ANY CRISIS
BY Dr BAK NGUYEN

THE LAZY FRANCHISE

089- **THE CONFESSION OF
A LAZY OVERACHIEVER**
BY Dr BAK NGUYEN

090- **TO OVERACHIEVE
EVERYTHING BEING LAZY**
CHEAT YOUR WAY TO SUCCESS
BY Dr BAK NGUYEN

PHILOSOPHY

003- **LEADERSHIP** -003
PANDORA'S BOX
BY Dr. BAK NGUYEN

015- **FORCES OF NATURE**
FORGING THE CHARACTER
OF WINNERS
BY Dr BAK NGUYEN

040- **KRYPTO**
TO SAVE THE WORLD
BY Dr. BAK NGUYEN & ILYAS BAKOUCH

ALPHA LADDERS 2 -081
SHAPING LEADERS AND ACHIEVERS
BY Dr BAK NGUYEN & BRENDA GARCIA

MIRROR -085
BY Dr BAK NGUYEN

099- **306 HAPPINESS QUOTES**
SHORTCUT VOLUME SEVEN
BY Dr. BAK NGUYEN

100- **170 DOCTOR QUOTES**
SHORTCUT VOLUME EIGHT
BY Dr. BAK NGUYEN

SHORTCUT

SOCIETY

408 HEALING QUOTES -093
SHORTCUT VOLUME ONE
BY Dr. BAK NGUYEN

408 GROWTH QUOTES -094
SHORTCUT VOLUME TWO
BY Dr. BAK NGUYEN

365 LEADERSHIP QUOTES -095
SHORTCUT VOLUME THREE
BY Dr. BAK NGUYEN

518 CONFIDENCE QUOTES -096
SHORTCUT VOLUME FOUR
BY Dr. BAK NGUYEN

317 SUCCESS QUOTES -097
SHORTCUT VOLUME FIVE
BY Dr. BAK NGUYEN

376 POWER QUOTES -098
SHORTCUT VOLUME SIX
BY Dr. BAK NGUYEN

013 - **LE RÊVE CANADIEN**
D'IMMIGRANT À MILLIONNAIRE
par DR BAK NGUYEN

054 - **CHOC**
LE JARDIN D'EDITH
par DR BAK NGUYEN

063 - **AFTERMATH**
BUSINESS AFTER THE GREAT PAUSE
BY Dr BAK NGUYEN & Dr ERIC LACOSTE

073 - **TOUCHSTONE**
LEVERAGING TODAY'S
PSYCHOLOGICAL SMOG
BY Dr BAK NGUYEN & Dr KEN SEROTA

074 - **COVIDCONOMICS**
THE GENERATION AHEAD
BY Dr BAK NGUYEN

THE POWER OF YES

THE POWER OF YES - 010
VOLUME ONE: IMPACT
BY Dr BAK NGUYEN

THE POWER OF YES 2 - 037
VOLUME TWO: SHAPELESS
BY Dr BAK NGUYEN

046 - **THE POWER OF YES 3**
VOLUME THREE: LIMITLESS
BY Dr BAK NGUYEN

087 - **THE POWER OF YES 4**
VOLUME FOUR: PURPOSE
BY Dr BAK NGUYEN

091 - **THE POWER OF YES 5**
VOLUME FIVE: ALPHA
BY Dr BAK NGUYEN

092 - **THE POWER OF YES 6**
VOLUME SIX: PERSPECTIVE
BY Dr BAK NGUYEN

TITLES AVAILABLE AT

www.DrBakNguyen.com

AMAZON - BARNES & NOBLE - APPLE BOOKS - KINDLE
SPOTIFY - APPLE MUSIC

www.ingramcontent.com/pod-product-compliance
Lightning Source LLC
LaVergne TN
LVHW051049080426
835508LV00019B/1789